Millionaire Mentality

A Compass to Success

Millionaire Mentality
ISBN
Copyright© 2016 by Tommy R. Twitty
Tommy R. Twitty Ministries
P.O. Box 613
Chesnee, SC 29323

Library of Congress Control Number: 2016900179

Millionaire Mentality

Table of Contents

Don't become like the people of this world. Instead, change the way you think. Then you will always be able to determine what God really wants—what is good, pleasing, and perfect.

(ROMANS 12:2 GW)

A Project of TRT Ministries

Summary Introduction
The Millionaire Mentality - A Compass to Success

Matthew 25:14-15 and 24-29 NLT

14"Again, the Kingdom of Heaven can be illustrated by the story of a man going on a long trip. He called together his servants and entrusted his money to them while he was gone. 15 He gave five bags of silver[b] to one, two bags of silver to another, and one bag of silver to the last—dividing it in proportion to their abilities. He then left on his trip.

24"Then the servant with the one bag of silver came and said, 'Master, I knew you were a harsh man, harvesting crops you didn't plant and gathering crops you didn't cultivate. 25 I was afraid I would lose your money, so I hid it in the earth. Look, here is your money back.' 26 "But the master replied, 'You wicked and lazy servant! If you knew I harvested crops I didn't plant and gathered crops I didn't cultivate,27 why didn't you deposit my money in the bank? At least I could have gotten some interest on it.' 28 "Then he ordered, 'Take the money from this servant, and give it to the one with the ten bags of silver. 29 To those who use well what they are given, even more will be given, and they will have an abundance. But from those who do nothing, even what little they have will be taken away.

Jesus uses this parable of the three servants to make numerous points about business, stewardship, and investing. It is the intent of this directional compass to successfully lead and guide you through this passage of scripture and the remaining scripture references from the standpoint of godly business, stewardship and investing both naturally and spiritually to help you obtain the mindset of a millionaire.

This road map to success will identify in the Word of God, the numerous times and places that Jesus operated in the capacity of a businessman and how he taught "man" lessons and instructions on how to obtain wealth. It is a road map to success, that will teach you how to navigate around and through opportunities, challenges and conflicts to get you to the place of managing your success.

It is a guide to naturally and spiritually obtaining wealth through the use of your own mind and the wisdom given to us in the form of the Bible. The Millionaire Mentality is a guided tour to teach you steps, stages and processes for obtaining the mindset or the mentality of a millionaire using the principals demonstrated during the time of Joseph, Nehemiah and others.

If you want to become a millionaire, you must change the way you think so you can change the way you live. A person is a millionaire because of how he or she thinks and how they respond to life's conflicts. Initiating, implementing and using the tools in this book will help to teach you to think like a millionaire who manages conflict, maintains success and achieves victories early on during the process.

Chapter 1
Five Talents
"Don't Hide or Bury your Gift"

Scripture Reference:

Matthew 25:14-30 NLT

14 "Again, the Kingdom of Heaven can be illustrated by the story of a man going on a long trip. He called together his Servants and entrusted his money to them while he was gone.

15 He gave Five Bags of silver to one, two bags of silver to another, and One Bag of silver to the last— dividing it in proportion to their Abilities. He then left on his trip.

16 "The Servant who received the Five Bags of silver began to invest the Money and earned five more.

17 The servant with Two Bags of silver also went to Work and earned two more.

18 But the Servant who received the One Bag of silver dug a hole in the ground and hid the Master's Money.

1st – Faithful Servant Talent

19 "After a long time their master returned from his trip and called them to give an Account (Report) of how they had used his money.

20 The servant to whom he had entrusted the Five Bags of silver came forward with five more and said, 'Master, you gave me Five Bags of silver to invest, and I have earned five more.'

21 "The master was full of praise. 'Well done, my good and Faithful Servant. You have been faithful in handling this small amount, so now I will give you many more responsibilities. Let's celebrate together!'

2nd - Faithful Servant Talent

22 "The Servant who had received the Two Bags of silver came forward and said, 'Master, you gave me Two Bags of silver to Invest, and I have earned two more.'

23 "The master said, 'Well done, my good and Faithful Servant. You have been Faithful in handling this small amount, so now I will give you many more responsibilities. Let's celebrate together!'

3rd - Unfaithful Servant Talent

24 "Then the Servant with the One Bag of silver came and said, 'Master, I knew you were a harsh man, harvesting crops you didn't plant and gathering crops you didn't cultivate.

25 I was afraid I would lose your money, so I hid it in the earth. Look, here is your money back.'

26 "But the master replied, 'You wicked and Lazy Servant! If you knew I harvested crops I didn't plant and gathered crops I didn't cultivate,

27 (WHY) didn't you deposit my money in the bank? At least I could have gotten some Interest   on it.'

28 "Then he ordered, 'Take the money from this Servant, and give it to the one with the ten   bags of silver.

29 To those who use well what they are given, even more will be given, and they will have an abundance. But from those who do nothing, even what little they have will be taken away.

30 Now throw this useless servant into outer darkness, where there will be weeping and gnashing of teeth.'

1st – Servant/Steward
He took five talents and doubled his profit.

2nd – Servant/Steward
He took two talents and doubled his profit.

3rd – Servant/Steward

He buried the one talent and made no profit.

Jesus' Investment

Jesus, the one who had sowed and invested into his servants, came back and audited his servants to see if there was a return or an increase on his investment.

Definition for Audit

To audit something or someone means to take an inspection of the accounting records and procedures of a business for the purpose of verifying the accuracy and completeness of the records and reports.

Jesus' Return on His Investment

Jesus came back and inspected His investor's, to see if each one had earned any interest or got a return on His investment.

There are three processes for how to manage the things in your life. The first process deals with responsibility, the second deals with accountability and the third credibility. All of these processes deal with how well you manage what Christ has given you.

Definition for Manage

The word manage means to take charge or to bring about or succeed in accomplishing, despite hardships or difficulty and to be motivated in spite of.

The Process of Responsibility

How to manage the responsibility of what God has gifted you to do.

The Process of Accountability

You must be accountable to your gift.

The Process of Credibility

Your gift must be credible, which means profitable, which means your gift has the ability to make a net profit because your gift is a product given by God. When your gift is profitable it can create a net profit of a 1,000 % return.

Hebrews 11:1 KJV
1 Now faith is the substance of things hoped for, the evidence of things not seen.

When Jesus returns to audit the servants with what He has given them. He promotes or gives more responsibility to the two servants that have caused an increase or a profit in their gifts or his money, and then Jesus promotes them from being a servant to being a ruler. Once they proved that they were good stewards, trustworthy, faithful and business minded. He turns around and says unto them you have been faithful over a few things but now I'm going to make you a ruler over many things.   Here you can see where God is really starting us off with a test run or a sample investment to see if He can make us investment partners or His equal partners in the Kingdom. The two servants moved from working for the company, empire, or the Kingdom, to now being investor's or partner's in the Kingdom.

The difference between a Servant and a Ruler.
1. A Servant is a borrower.
2. A Ruler is a lender.

<u>Millionaire Mindset or Mentality</u>
We cannot think like the last servant or steward that took his gift, his ability, and his investment and buried it in the ground. He buried his gift because he didn't understand the difference between credit and success. We must think like the two good servants/stewards that made double on their investments.

We have been taught in America, that we are to work real hard and build good credit, when the truth is, credit is designed for poor people. Assets and capital are designed for rich people. As long as you have capital and assets; despite if your credit score is beneath 500; you can still build million dollar buildings. Donald Trump has learned the principles of how to invest his money and not to bury his money. When you're not investing money, it's not accumulating, growing, increasing or multiplying, so your money serves no purpose.

Money is a seed, such as an apple, orange or an oak tree. It starts off by just being a simple seed, it grows over time, develops and becomes something fruitful and purposeful. Money is designed to do the same thing, be fruitful and to serve a purpose.

Talent
A talent is not a coin, it is a weight.

Definition of Weight
Weight represents a measure, which means a measurement of value. In finances, an evaluation is the process of estimating the potential market value of a financial asset or liability.

Talents Worth of Wages

A talent was worth a year's wages. But a bag of talent was worth 20 year's wages. The Greek word for talent is (kikkar), which means a measure of weight or worth money. When you discover your talent, it reveals your value or worth in money.

The 1st - Faithful Servant was given five talents or five bags of weighted money. Each talent was worth 20 years wages. Every generation equals 20 years. Jesus gave the 1st - servant a 100 years worth of wages because 5 X 20 = 100.

The 1st - Faithful Servant doubled his wages to 10 talents: 10 X 20 = 200 years worth of wages, which now is enough to support 10 generations: 10 X 20 = 200 years worth of wages or investments.

The 2nd - Faithful Servant had 2 talents. Each talent represents 20 years worth of wages. So he started with 40 years wages / investments, because 2 x 20 = 40, which equals two generations.

The 2nd - Faithful Servant doubled his profit and now he has increased his new wages to 80 years in profit, because 4 X 20 = 80 years worth of wages, which now equals enough to support four generations.

The 3rd - Unfaithful Servant had 1 talent which equaled 20 years worth of wages or one generation. This means 20 years later, the servant who had buried his talent, investment, and ability for 20 years did not increase or make a profit to be laid up for another generation. The Unfaithful Servant took a 20 year investment and wasted it. (1x20=20 Loss yrs. = failure).

The 3rd – Unfaithful Servant who Jesus called lazy, trifling and full of excuses took his investment and buried the investment in the ground for 20 years, without doing anything with it. He allowed the talent, his gift, and the ability that Jesus invested to go to waste for 20 years of his life, without doing anything with it; and 20 years later Jesus came and audited the report on this lazy unfaithful servant and the excuses the unfaithful servant gave Jesus was he was afraid to use the investment, gift, and the ability he had been given. So he decided for 20 years to take his investment and bury it; doing nothing with it to bring a return.

Jesus called this man lazy and wicked and he stripped him by repossessing the investment, the gift, and the ability that He had favored this unfaithful servant to possess over 20 years. By taking the talent and re-investing the one talent into the faithful servant that had proven he could multi-task, had multi-purpose and most of all he would be profitable by expanding the brand.

Jesus did the Audit Report

When Jesus came to inspect he looked for checks and balances and it was determined that this servant was spending and wasting in his present and that he did not invest in his future, for his children's children. What type of investor do you want to be?

There are only 2 types of investors.

The 1st – is called Atychiphobia Mentality.

The 2nd – is called F.O.M.O. Investor Mentality.

Atychiphobia means Fear of Failure. This type of investor always fails at succeeding in life.

The unfaithful servant, that Jesus called lazy and wicked, suffered from Atychiphobia, the Fear of Failure. So, he buried his opportunity to be successful by not using his gift, talent, and ability to succeed in life.

The 2nd - Type is called F.O.M.O. Investor Mentality. F.O.M.O. means (fear of missing out).

The 2 Faithful Servants that Jesus invested into, operated out of an F.O.M.O. Investor Mentality. They had a fear of missing out; not on being successful but they had a fear of missing out on being an entrepreneur and they had a fear of missing out on not being an over-comer; but being more than a conqueror. They had a fear of not growing their money, or growing their business. This F.O.M.O. Investor Mentality caused them not to develop people, product and processes to franchise an enterprise, or to prepare for the next generation to be successful.

The Unfaithful Servant struggled from Atychiphobia, Fear of Failure and buried the investment, the gift and the ability to be successful.

In this season, as well as the seasons to come your Mentality will be that you're no longer operating with Atychiphobia, Fear of Failure, but you're going to live your life with F.O.M.O. fear of missing out on what life and God has Promised You! Don't confuse talents with purpose. Too many people confuse their talent and gift with what they want to do in life. But purpose reveals what you are created to do in life. The reason the 2 Faithful Servants were successful with doubling their investment, was because they had a purpose and process for their assignment. The Unfaithful Servant buried his investment, because he was given a talent and gift without understanding his purpose for his investment. Once you find your passion you find your purpose, but it is also possible to be passionate about something you're not good at.

EXAMPLE: "American Idol", has many people that try out or audition to sing, and they're not good at it. They have a passion to sing, but they don't have a purpose or gift to be successful. That's why they are voted off, without making it past the first round auditions. They had a passion without purpose.

When Jesus came back from His long journey which was equivalent to 20 years or longer to audit a report from all three servants, they had to give an accountability report, a responsibility report and a creditability report, of what they had done with Jesus' investment.

Chapter 2

<u>INCREASING FAVOR / TRIPLE FAVOR</u>

Each place that God brings you into creates a new level or dimension of favor over your life. Isaac experienced triple favor over his life.

Genesis 26:13 NKJV
The man began to prosper and continued prospering until he became very prosperous.

<u>New Attraction & Wells</u>
When the process takes place where we have broken the backbone of poverty, we create what is called a "New Attraction". The "New Attraction" is where we begin to attract our haters.

<u>"Wells" represent 3 things in the Spirit</u>
The first thing a "well" represents is a place of resource. Resource provides a source of income and security. The second thing that "wells" represent is a place of provision and third a place of blessing. In Genesis 26:15, if Isaac had left Egypt, as Abimelech had instructed he would have left his place of resource, provision & blessing. Wells not only

represent resource, provision, and blessing; but they also represent truth.

Isaac was attacked by the enemy in 3 places.

- Gerar - This place represents a place of circle or cycle. It means a place of wandering. The enemy always tries to take advantage of a believer when the believer is wandering in a day of old cycle and old season.

- Esek - This place means a place of contention, strife and jealousy.

- Sitnah - This place represents a place of hostility, anger and hatred.

Isaac came to a place called Rehoboth. Rehoboth represents...

- A place of enlargement.
- A place called more than enough.
- A place called increase.
- A place where God enlarges your territory.

The Law of Sowing and Reaping

This is the first of the Universal Laws. It's known as the "Law of Cause and Effect" and is defined as what you sow, being the cause and what you reap is the effect. In other words you cannot plant one type of seed and produce a different type of harvest; that's the law.

The Law of Germination

This law says whatever is planted requires some time before it comes into fruition. Every idea or anything you plant requires a certain action and a certain amount of time before the outcome is realized. You need to sow your ideas, allow them to germinate, give them a lot of energy, and then you will reap your reward.

In the unconscious mind (the negative) The seed produces seed so that when the conscious mind becomes awake or aware of what should have produced a harvest of millions, it realizes that it has produced a harvest of doubt (weed), that has left you broke. This is called the Law of Germination.

The Human Body

The human body or our trilogy, is made up of three parts. These three parts represent spirit, body and soul and the whole makes up a human life.
In the human body, all three parts relate and send messages to the mind, which is made up of 3 parts; the conscious, the unconscious and the subconscious, all three are one. The Spirit serves

God, the Soul serves the Spirit and the body serves the Soul.

The seed that was sown represented the world and the world represents three things.

1st it represents the physical world (fleshly mind) --- conscious mind.

2nd - It represents the mental world, the mental world is the (soul mind) ---unconscious mind.

3rd - It represents the spiritual world (spiritual mind) --- subconscious mind.

The principle of good and truth are implanted in the interior part of man's mind, but man has not tapped into 90% of his mind's abilities he has only tapped into the flesh, which is 10%. God has promised to the spiritual mind, a harvest, A Millionaire Mentality.

- 1st – Stage: He first formed man from the dirt that became flesh (conscious mind), which was the image. Because image means negative, flesh was always the negative of man.

- 2nd - Stage: God breathed into man (His Spirit), which gave man a Spiritual Mind (subconscious mind), which became God's likeness, which represents (positive) thoughts.

- 3rd - Stage: Man became a living soul (unconscious mind), which produced the trilogy 3 in 1; which in turn produced "Zoe" (a God kind of life or living).

Many of us are in a season where God is creating a Millionaire Mentality. Throughout the season He has exposed people, your so-called friends, your so-called connections, and your so-called covenants that are in your life. God has been trying to separate you but now the wheat and the tare must grow up together. What we were not willing to separate from ourselves, God is going to separate for us. That's why God in this season of double favor and manifestation, is exposing every relationship, companionship, and friendship, that doesn't belong in this season or in this stage of your life.

In the beginning stages of growth there is a similarity or resemblance between wheat and tare. In the beginning stage of sowing for your harvest you could not tell the difference between the wheat and the tare, they look very much alike, but in the maturing stage or the final stage (reaping) there is a big difference between the wheat and the tare, they no longer look alike.

Wheat in its Final Stage

The wheat becomes whiter; the tare in its final stage becomes darker. The bigger the wheat becomes the more it bends, it becomes more prostrate, more humble. It represents worship, which says the more God blesses it and multiplies it, the more humble it becomes.

Tare in its Final Stage

Tare does the opposite. Not only does it become darker or blacker, but the bigger tare becomes, the more it stands straight up, the more poisonous it becomes, the more dangerous it becomes, and the more arrogant it becomes. So to each and every one of us, if we are going to adventure out any further and take on this millionaire mentality, each one of us needs to ask ourselves this simple question?
CAN YOU STAND TO BE BLESSED?

Chapter 3
This Time I'm Not Coming Out Empty-Handed!"

This time I'm not coming out empty-handed deals with a mental mindset which represents choice, not chance, and it determines your destiny.

In the Iceberg Theory the conscious mind represents the tip of the Iceberg; the part we use the most, which represents the 10 % of our brain that we are using. The bulk represents the unconscious part of the brain which represents the 90% that we don't use or see. This means our mentality is only used at 10% of our capacity to think and the other 90% we haven't even tapped into. So, that's why we can't understand the return of the 10% tithes and the other 90% that God gives back to us. When we learn how to tap into the unconscious mind, then we will start understanding how to tap into the 90% of abundant living.

Changing the way you think
The Egyptians gave their gold and silver to the Hebrews (the people of God), and they came out of Egypt as Multi-Millionaires.

Psalms 105:37 NLT
37 The Lord brought his people out of Egypt, loaded with silver and gold; and not one among the tribes of Israel even stumbled.

In other words, the Lord brought his people out of Egypt loaded with silver and gold and not one of them struggled, or was impoverished, which means, not one came out broke. The reason for this is because the Israelites won the civil lawsuit that says if the thief be found he must pay back 7- Fold which means 7- Fold Blessing.

Proverbs 6:31 NLT
31 But if he is caught, he must pay back seven times what he stole, even if he has to sell everything in his house.

Just like God gave Abraham a covenant of a 7-Fold blessing, when we find the one that was allowed to rob our generation, which represented seven generations of lineage and everything that was lost, we will receive the seven generations' before us blessings.

The people of God were dealing with a mentality problem when it came to getting out of Egypt. The man of God was leading the People of God out of Egypt as millionaires; each family was leaving as millionaires, but they still had a poverty and broken mentality. They had accomplished bankrupting the richest powers of the world and they were still talking about turning around, let's go back and see if Pharaoh will give us our old job back. The job they wanted to go back to was a minimum wage job, but they were already millionaires. They were millionaires but they still thought like slaves, broken people, and people of bondage because their mindset had not changed. The Word of Deliverance Church Motto is: **If You Change The Way You Think, You Will Change The Way You Live.** The Hebrews needed to change the way they were thinking so they could recognize that they were already millionaires.

Successful People (vs.) Unsuccessful People

- Successful people learn and grow so they can learn and grow more; because they are open-minded and transparent.

- Unsuccessful people, never learn anymore because they think that they already know everything and they are closed minded.

- Successful people act or do in spite of fear.

- Unsuccessful people always let fear stop them.

- Successful people see every dollar as a seed that can grow and make more money.

- Unsuccessful people see every dollar as a bill that causes more debt and this is why they struggle to have money. They see investing in their future as a bad investment, so they keep investing in their past and present liabilities.

Mephibosheth is the son of a King, and a part of the royal family; but he has been broken, dropped in life, and left crippled. This accident has not only left him physically broken, but he is also mentally broken. He has a broken mentality which has left him socially broken and he does not have a nickel to his name, when he has been left millions. Now, King David comes forth to deliver him and bring him back into the Kingdom and connect him back with the royal family. At the end, Mephibosheth is delivered, but he's still broken. The reason he's still broken is because of what he keeps tolerating through each season.

Tolerate

Tolerate means to put up with; to practice how to do without; it means to have a tolerance, which means a legal permission to keep taking in more of what makes you become numb in thinking and doing and it has the potential to produce a prodigal life. The prodigal son began to join people that tolerated him in a season instead of being connected with people who celebrate with him in his season. When he connected to the people that tolerated him, he took on a poverty mentality, which means he connected with people that didn't hold him accountable, responsible, or credible. When you connect with this type of people like the prodigal son did, it will cause you to lose everything.

Luke 15: 17-18 NKJV

17 "But when he came to himself, he said, 'How many of my father's hired servants have bread enough and to spare, and I perish with hunger! 18 I will arise and go to my father, and will say to him, "Father, I have sinned against heaven and before you.

The Prodigal Son and the 6 Senses.

- **Perception**- deals with how you perceive reality. It is our reality check. Conception deals with what you are birthing or producing. When you don't understand the power of conception you end up with the power of deception. (Genesis 3)

- **Imagination** - deals with creative ideas and the ability to dream.

- **Will-power**- is the power to mentally focus on your goal and be able to overcome any denials or setbacks.

- **Intuition** - is the mental faculty that helps you pick up information that is uncertain, but sure.

- **Memory** - deals with training the conscious mind (your thoughts) to retrieve lost and important information that has been downloaded through the years that you cannot afford to lose.

- **Reason/the voice of reason** deals with the inner voice that becomes vocal or audible. This voice of reason is how you decide to be. It's what helps you to decide to become who you are. It's what you decide to have, what you decide to do, what you decide to be and by all reason, what you want in life.

The first thing he (the Prodigal son) did was to get a perception on where he was in life. He came to himself and realized that his perception was reality. This meant that deception had set in and caused him to be deceived about reality. Then the voice of reason spoke and he declared out loud so that now what he thought of doing, he decided to do and what he decided to do he began to do. Then his imagination kicks in and he begins to dream and to visualize and while visualizing his memory kicks in. His conscious mind goes back and gathers from his mind the important information that he had thought was lost. The Bible said he remembered which means he went back in his memory and retrieved the thoughts that gave him will-power or the mental power that helped to get his focus back on his goals. Once he got his focus back again he remembered, in his memory, that he was a part of a real covenant relationship and that he should not have been in this state of mind of being busted and disgusted, living in poverty when he had been raised in a relationship and covenant with a millionaire mentality that gives him a millionaire status.

At last his intuition kicked in and he said to himself; I will rise and go to my father's house because like will-power, our intuition helps us to pick-up the information that has left us uncertain and confused and it helps us to get our swagger back. Your intuition combined with your will-power helps you to get your confidence back, your certainty back and it makes you get up and go get what is rightfully yours. When the prodigal son quit being lost, he understood that he had regained the millionaire mentality. His father gave him back the millionaire status and put on him some clothes like Louis Vuitton and Gucci. He had tailor made suits put on him, shoes that were like crocodiles, alligators or ostrich and then he turned around and put on him a 24 carat gold ring. In addition to this, his father threw him a house party and they started playing *Kool and The Gang's* song *"It's a Celebration"*.

That's why Egypt was so blessed in the beginning because Pharaoh blessed Joseph and blessed the people of God, but when he started trying to take from the people of God, God began to curse Egypt and Pharaoh. This is when Moses tried to introduce to the people a millionaire mentality and to let them know you no longer have to work minimum wage jobs without benefits, without appreciation, without security, but now you can rise up and take on the mentality that you are the head and not the tail. You are above and not beneath, you are a lender and not a borrower. If God be for you, He's more than this world against you. He wanted them to know my God shall supply all of your needs according to his riches in glory. You are God's little children and greater is He that is in you than he that is in the world. If you abide in Him and he abide in you, you can ask what you will and it shall be given unto you; for what the devil meant for your evil, God meant for your good; and now no weapon formed against you shall be able to prosper. For it is the Lord who has given you this power to get this wealth (millions) and not ye yourself.

A WORD OF DECLARATION & DECREE

I refuse to come out of this season with nothing, as I went in with nothing, I'm coming out with everything; I went in poor, but I'm coming out rich; I went in sick, but I'm coming out healed; I went in with my head down, but I'm coming out with my head up; I went in without, but I'm coming out with everything. I will gather my strength and reasoning to make an ultimate and final decision to be who God says that I am, to do what God said I could do and my ultimate reason or decision is to tell the devil I changed my mind. He can have everything he's given me back, but everything I've lost to him, I'm taking it all back! Finally in this declaration, tell the devil. You have got to go! Because as God told Moses to tell pharaoh "let my people go" and restore back to them; You will restore back the 7-Fold Blessing and the 7-Fold payback of everything you've taken from me.

Chapter 4

The 5 Laws of Manifestation

The 5 Laws of Manifestation

1st - The Law of Passion
2nd - The Law of Intention
3rd - The Law of Accumulation
4th - The Law of Creativity
5th - The Law of Exchange

1st - The Law of Passion

If you are going to be effective in doing things for the Kingdom, from a millionaire mentality, you must first start with the law of passion. The law of passion means that all actions, including prosperity related actions are motivated by emotion. Success at any level or endeavor requires an emotional charge. You have to feel the fire of desire to reach challenging goals. In other words the actions that lead to what you want are always fueled by passion.

The first thing Jesus did, was to operate with the law of passion. Jesus looked with passion and compassion and saw that the multitude of people that were in the desert and he saw that they were hungry or starving and he used passion to begin the strategic thinking of Kingdom Ministry.

Mark 6:34

34 When Jesus landed and saw a large crowd, he had (PASSION) on them, because they were like sheep without a shepherd.

Which meant that whoever was over them was not shepherding them because they were like sheep without shepherd.

2nd - The Law of Intention

You are most likely to manifest what you focus on intently. You attract into your life the people and opportunities that reflect your dominant thoughts and intentions. The Law of Intention when working together with the Law of Passion draws strength and energy from your positive thinking. When you carefully cultivate certain thoughts and energize them with passion, you tend to attract what you need to turn those thoughts into a tangible reality. Intention means to aim, plan or strategize. It sees a problem and begins to rationalize the solution to the problem.

3rd - Law of Accumulation

Anything of value is the result of many small efforts that eventually add up to something bigger over time. In other words, you reap what you sow; for everything that happens, there are a series of small actions that caused it to happen. We all have the ability to respond, we all have choices and those choices have consequences. We are very active participants in creating the conditions of our lives. We are accountable and everything counts.

Accumulation means to gather together or acquire, an increasing number of quantities. It means to multiply, to increase, or to capitalize more quantity in numbers. It means to build up and to grow. When the disciples brought back 2 fish and 5 loaves of bread they operated with the law of accumulation.

Mark 6:41 NIV
41 Taking the five loaves and the two fish and looking up to heaven, he gave thanks and broke the loaves. Then he gave them to his disciples to distribute to the people. He also divided the two fish among them all.

Matthew 15:37a AMP
37 They all ate and were satisfied.

4ᵗʰ - The Law of Creativity

This law deals with how to take a problem and work at the problem until it becomes the solution. It deals with how to visualize what you don't see in the natural (conscious) mind, but see in the spiritual (subconscious) mind. It also deals with calling those things as though they are not, as though they are. Becoming a problem solver, this means becoming a solution to the problem, not a problem to the solution.

Romans 4:17b KJV
17 Even God, who quickeneth the dead, and calleth those things which be not as though they were.

Jesus saw the solution to the problem and He declared the end from the beginning, because he that began a good work in you will always complete it at His appearing (Manifestation). That's why you should never despise your days of small beginnings.

5ᵗʰ - The Law of Exchange
The Law of Exchange is the most important of all. The Laws of Manifestation state that we must continually exchange something of importance with others.

For example, when resources exchange, their value increases, if the exchange is mutually beneficial, the relationship flourishes and facilitates more and further exchange. The value of resources continues to increase.

Isaiah 60:17 NLT
17 I will exchange your bronze for gold, your iron for silver, your wood for bronze, and your stones for iron. I will make peace your leader and righteousness your ruler.

Isaiah 61:3 NKJV
3 To console those who mourn in Zion, to give them beauty for ashes, The oil of joy for mourning, The garment of praise for the spirit of heaviness; That they may be called trees of righteousness, The planting of the Lord, that He may be glorified."

What Jesus did to close out feeding the 5,000. He operated in the Law of Exchange.

In Business Translation......Jesus Did 4 Things:
1st – Product: He saw the product (people) and he invested in the product.

- **2nd – Market:** He used a marketing strategy to market his ministry.

- **3rd – Manufacture:** The process of converting raw material, which represents substance into a finished product. Substance is all you need to start a business or to be successful.

Hebrew 11:1 NKJV
11 Now faith is the substance of things hoped for, the evidence of things not seen.

When your raw thoughts can produce substance, it will produce evidence. What you may be doing right now is raw, it may be in its intangible stage, but if you learn how to manufacture and to convert what you think into what you believe, you can manifest a reality into existence.

- **4th – Distribute:** Jesus took the 12 disciples and used them to distribute and feed over 5,000 people. He himself became a distribution center. Distribution is the act of distributing or moving the finished product; it's the process of moving the finished product from the manufacturing source to its customers.

Jesus had to teach them the business principles of marketing and manufacturing to get them to the law of exchange. The law of exchange and the law of creativity work hand in hand.

John 6:13 KJV
13 Therefore they gathered them together, and filled twelve baskets with the fragments of the five barley loaves, which remained over and above unto them that had eaten.

The word fragments is a Jewish word that means increasing capacity, it does not mean scraps or leftovers or fragments like in the English translation. Each basket can hold 30 loaves in each one. 12 X 30 = 360 + the 5 loaves the boy started with in the beginning = 365. What happened when they took up the baskets in the end, Jesus left them a message.

- **The 1st - thing Jesus does is bless it.**

- **The 2nd - thing Jesus does is break it.** Which is an indication that you were blessed before you were broken. No matter how life tries to break you over and over again, always remember you were blessed by Jesus first.

 No more boundaries, we are operating in the law of accumulation. So what was immature, as soon as Jesus breaks it, it becomes mature, it multiplies and increases in interest.

In some places of our lives, we did not grow, we did not improve, we did not become stronger or wiser until what we went through broke us and took the limits off of us. Then we moved from a place of limitations to a place called destination.

The bread represents revelation and the fish or the meat represents maturity and Jesus understood that if we were going to get more revelation, we had to be at a place where we ate more meat to get to a place of maturity.

1 Corinthians 3:2 NLT
2 I had to feed you with milk, not with solid food, because you weren't ready for anything stronger. And you still aren't ready.

Hebrews 5:12 NLT
12 You have been believers so long now that you ought to be teaching others. Instead, you need someone to teach you again the basic things about God's word. You are like babies who need milk and cannot eat solid food.

Jesus took these 5 Laws of Manifestation and these 4 business principles and led a people from a place of not enough, to a place called more than enough because he applied these laws and the principles.

Chapter 5

The Millionaire Next Door

<u>Topic Scripture:</u> 2 Kings 4:1-7 NLT

One day the widow of a member of the group of prophets came to Elisha and cried out, "My husband who served you is dead, and you know how he feared the LORD. But now a creditor has come, threatening to take my two sons as slaves." ² "What can I do to help you?" Elisha asked. "Tell me, what do you have in the house?" "Nothing at all, except a flask of olive oil," she replied. ³ And Elisha said, "Borrow as many empty jars as you can from your friends and neighbors. ⁴ Then go into your house with your sons and shut the door behind you. Pour olive oil from your flask into the jars, setting each one aside when it is filled." ⁵ So she did as she was told. Her sons kept bringing jars to her, and she filled one after another. ⁶ Soon every container was full to the brim! "Bring me another jar," she said to one of her sons. "There aren't any more!" he told her. And then the olive oil stopped flowing. [7] When she told the man of God what had happened, he said to her, "Now sell the olive oil and pay your debts, and you and your sons can live on what is left over."

The Bible starts off by telling us about this family. The woman's husband was a man of God. He reverenced and loved God, he was a part of the covenant, and he was a Spiritual son to Elisha, but he was in debt. He was not good at handling business and he was not business minded.

Proverbs 13:22 NKJV
22 A good man leaves an inheritance to his children's children, but the wealth of the sinner is stored up for the righteous.

Proverbs 13:22 NLT
22 Good people leave an inheritance to their grandchildren, but the sinner's wealth passes to the godly.

2 Corinthians 12:14 NKJV
14 Now for the third time I am ready to come to you. And I will not be burdensome to you; for I do

**not seek yours, but you. For the children ought
not to lay up for the parents, but the parents for
the children.**

3 reasons this family was left in debt.

In order to establish what's called wealth, money and
influence, those that have wealth, money and
influence (such as banks and other lending
institutions) have to evaluate 3 criteria before they do
any type of business with you.

1st - They check out your Stability.
2nd - They check out your Liability.
3rd - They check out your Credibility.

Stability deals with something or someone being
stable or solid. At this particular time this woman had
no stability in her life; which means nothing of quality;
strength and endurance.

Liability means a state of being responsible for
something or someone; a debt or financial obligation.
It means to be liable, which means you're taking the
responsibility for something or someone if it goes
wrong. They go back and check your previous
history, such as how long you've been working or
how long you've been on that job. They look at how

well you've been doing with those you've previously been in debt too.

Credibility means the quality of being trusted; means to be credited; means to be capable or believable, dependable and able or good enough to pay off or take care of a particular thing or debt. How you've paid off previous debt and the interest you've previously accumulated. These lenders are looking for a high credit score.

The first thing the woman had to do was to understand the millionaire mentality. How to transform into a virtuous woman with a millionaire mentality; by understanding she couldn't afford to lose her kids to DSS, the streets, drugs, crime, or to an occult. But now she had to come up with a plan. So, the man of God speaks a prophetic word in her life by asking, what was in her house? She then moved from being an unemployed broken housewife to taking on an entrepreneur mindset. She is not only willing to be a hearer of the Word of God, but now she would be a doer of the Word of God, by discovering what was in her house. In her house she discovered her gift, which was the oil. The oil represented her purpose in life that will now bring stability back into her life and she will no longer live her life as a liability, but now she will gain credibility by starting her own business.

Proverbs 18:16 KJV
16 A man's Gift maketh room for him, and bringeth him before great men.

Proverbs 18:16 NLT
16 Giving a gift can open doors; it gives access to important people!

When the woman opened her gift (favor), doors opened for her. She is now able to go into her community and borrow vessels that she once couldn't borrow. She gained credibility with people of greatness and of great riches, when she begin to understand her value because of her oil (gift) that was in the house. The oil became her collateral or equity and what she put up for her investors' investment, It gave her assets and credibility and those of credibility and influence extended her credit by investing into her their empty vessels because now they knew her value.

When you go to get a bank loan....
- The 1st - thing they do is pull your credit history to see if you are a liability or a risk or if you

have the credit to receive the loan you're asking for

- The 2nd - thing they want to know is what you are going to use for collateral to help prove and determine whether or not if you receive approval of the loan, if they are willing to invest and over time can you protect the interest of the loan that deals with your future.

An investment is only geared to build and to protect future deals. It does not deal with the right now or the present. We must stop looking for a new day, but look for a new time.

4 Processes/Instructions for Developing Your Gift

The 1st process: He helped her to discover her gift. The oil represented her gift and the value that was in the house. He helped her to understand the value and wealth of her purpose in life and to understand her net- worth. Once you know and understand your gift, your value and your net-worth, then you are able to partner up and network with others that understand and know their gift, their value and their net-worth.

2 Kings 4:2 AMP
2 Elisha said to her, what shall I do for you? Tell me, what have do you have to sale/or of value in

your house? She said your handmaid has nothing in the house except a jar of oil.

The 2nd process: He helped her to <u>manage her gift</u>. He instructed her to get her sons to go out and borrow vessels from those who would become investors in her vision.

To manage means to maintain, to be good stewards. To be the manager and to be responsible over what has been given to you. What you have been given power and authority to rule over; to maintenance. Therefore, people that are going to net-work with you have to be good stewards or they cannot be a part of the managing process.   There are people that are connected to your destiny, but quit connecting with people that are not a part of your destiny nor are they going in the same direction that you are going in.

 The 3rd process: The woman was taught how to <u>market her gift</u>. To market means to advertise, to promote or to endorse something. It is the responsibility of the management process to identify, anticipate, and satisfy customers by targeting their interest. This simply means the ability to know where you are today, to know where you would like to be in the future, and to make adjustments along the way will determine your value. Where you stand today and where your goals are for tomorrow, will also help to determine your future value.

Example:

Blockbuster was the top video company in the nation and they had to file bankruptcy because they stopped marketing and managing for tomorrow. They became over confident about their yesterday. They didn't see another company rising up out of a place called nowhere by the name of Netflix. Who eventually began to outgrow Blockbuster. It was indicated that at one time, Netflix went to Blockbuster and tried to sell them their company for 50 million dollars, but because Blockbuster was overconfident, they turned down the offer, and now Netflix is worth billions. The same one they rejected is now the most thriving video company in the world.

Blockbuster's mindset was just to rent/sell videos and make money off late fees and their customers, but Netflix came up with a new solution that created more revenues or money by allowing customers to go and pick up movies without late fees and make up revenues in other ways. Netflix was willing to think outside the box, while Blockbuster wasn't willing to make adjustments.

Example: Domino's recognized it couldn't keep up with Pizza Hut and Pizza Inn and that it was about to go out of business. However, they made adjustments to compete against Pizza Hut and Pizza Inn. They began offering delivery services. They made it easier for the customer, even though Pizza Hut and Pizza Inn may have been better. They discovered that people buy out of convenience rather than inconvenience. When you make things easier for the customers, they will always buy into what you're selling. This is simply good marketing and good business.

The 4th process: The woman was taught how to <u>sell her gift</u>.

2 Kings 4:7 GNB
7 She went back to Elisha, the prophet, who said to her, sell the olive oil and pay all your debts, and there will be enough money left over for you and your sons to live on.

The woman had already discovered, managed and marketed her gift and now she was ready to sell it and profit millions off her gift. She was a Millionaire the whole time but she didn't know what was in her house. The people next door didn't even know they had a Millionaire living right next door. You may be living in the projects, in a low income housing community, or you may be living in a trailer park, or right now you may be homeless and living in someone else's house; but once you discover what's in your house, the Bible declares inside these broken vessels are hidden treasures (Millions).

One day, she experienced the death of her husband, the next day she experienced her debtors, bill collectors, the bank was foreclosing on her house and land, they were ready to come and repossess all of her property and ready to take her sons and make slaves out of them, and put them in a system where they would become just another number. The woman started a business when she was at a place where she was about to lose everything, only to become the millionaire next door. She went from being unemployed, to being a successful entrepreneur within a few days; not having money one day, to being a millionaire the next day. She went from foreclosure, bankruptcy, and repossession, to owning an empire. She went from about to lose her house one day, to paying it off. She moved from debt cancellation to the transformation of wealth.

You're about to get off the exit too early and turn around and go back because you think you are lost in debt, but go on up to the next exit and get off, it's called Financial Freedom and keep straight. All her neighbors saw foreclosure signs up in her yard, her land being listed in the paper getting ready to be auctioned off, but she came back and bought the whole block. Simply because she stopped thinking poverty, broken mentality, and thinking like a loser. She stopped thinking defeated and began to take on a millionaire mentality. She went from using oil and, buying oil, to producing oil, marketing oil, manufacturing oil, distributing oil, and to selling oil. She became the millionaire next door because she quit thinking like her block, her environment, her neighborhood, and began to change it.

She stopped being part of the problem and became part of the solution. She moved from being a part of the "have nots" to a part of the "haves". She moved from not enough, then passed just enough, to more than enough, all because she discovered if you can see it, you can sell it, but if you can't see it, you will just keep buying it.

WHAT'S IN YOUR HOUSE?

Chapter 6
8 Steps to Success

Psalms 37:23 NKJV
23 The steps of a good man are ordered by the Lord, and He delights in his way.

Elisha followed Elijah's steps of success in 2nd Kings, chapter 2. He became the successor to his predecessor and received a double portion of success. He was willing to follow the steps to success and he became successful. You have to understand that in order to become successful you have to know the process of success, but in order to truly become successful you have to plan and prepare for it. Success just does not happen on its own. It does not come by coincidence or happenstance. Success is not something someone can place on you even though you can become a successor. It's only when you have been proven you are a successor and that you are able to follow in someone else's steps of success that makes you successful.

8 steps that make up Success and makes one Successful.

The 1st - Step to success is Passion.

Passion simply means fulfillment completing one's emptiness and void by the same passion that God had in the beginning when He saw the world that was in darkness with emptiness and void. His passion looked past the darkness and void and said, *"Let there be light."* So, passion caused the darkness all around you to create a light that's inside of you to come forward.

In Genesis we learn about Joseph. Joseph had passion and he was a dreamer. The Bible says, according to Genesis chapters 37-39, Joseph went through the making of success process. Whenever you go through the process of becoming successful it will always cause you to experience **CRAP**. (C.R.A.P.)

C. R. A. P.

- Joseph was Criticized for being a dreamer.
- Joseph was Rejected by his brothers.

- Adversary: Joseph was hated by his brothers. His brothers also tried to kill him and by throwing him in the pit and leaving him for dead.
- Joseph stayed Persistent through Criticism, Rejection, Adversity, by being hated, by being thrown in the pit and by being sold as a slave to the enemy. (Ishmaelite)

The 2nd - Step to Success is Work.

In order to be successful you've got to work at it. (2 Thessalonians 3:10 KJV & 2 Thessalonians 3:10-13 MSG) Work is the second step to being successful. You have to have the ability to work in hostile environments such as a job, home, ministry, or community.

Nehemiah 4:6 NKJV
6 So we built the wall, and the entire wall was joined together up to half its height, for the people had a mind to work.

The people that rebuilt the wall still rose up to build because they had a mind to work. The Bible says in Genesis chapter one, God became self-employed, founder, C.E.O, architect and master builder over His own company called heaven and earth. He began to laying out the blueprint and He completed the construction on earth in 6 days. The Bible says, He worked and did not stop working until the 6th day. Then He completed the work on the 7th day, God retired from something He finished and not something He started and did not finish. Too many times the reason many don't reach their complete capacity of fulfillment called success is because we start something without finishing it. We've got to learn to work it until we finish it!

The 3rd – Step to Success is to Stay Focused.
Matthew 14:28-30 GW

28 Peter answered, "Lord, if it is you, order me to Peter answered, to you on the water."

29 Jesus said, "Come!" So Peter got out of the boat and walked on the water toward Jesus.

30 But when he noticed how strong the wind was, he became afraid and started to sink. He shouted, "Lord, save me!"

Psalms 37:23 NKJV

23 His steps were being ordered; which means Jesus had ordered his steps to success that caused Peter to do the impossible but when he lost his focus he went from success back to failure.

As long as you're walking in the steps of success you're not focusing on the storm; you're focusing on your assignment but when you focus more on your storms then your assignments; you're going to always end up at a place like Peter. Peter ended up farther from success and closer to failure rather than farther from failure and closer to success.

When you lose your focus you lose the power and favor that goes with it. As long as Peter was focused, he had power and favor to walk in the supernatural and to do the supernatural but when he lost his focus he lost his supernatural ability of power and favor. Focus deals with attitude, stability and perseverance.

Staying focused empowers you. It gives you power & favor but losing focus takes you away from being able to do the impossible and brings you back to a place called mediocre/average. A loss of focus causes you to lose focus of your assignment. Your assignment is the only thing that empowers you and favors you to be successful because your steps are ordered by God.

The 4th – Step to success is to Push Yourself.
Push yourself simply means to press through, to move pass and overcome any situation or circumstance. Push also means that it's not where you start, it's how you finish! You must be willing to push yourself! The Bible say, the woman with the issue of blood pushed herself by pressing through the crowd and this caused her situation to change into success. She was told for 12 years that she could not, and should not, and cannot do because of her

situation and her issues in life. She pushed through the crowd after 12 years and found success.

The woman with the issue of blood after 12 years became successful over all the issues that she had failed at for 12 years. It was only when she decided to deal with her issues and push herself pass her issues that her issues changed after 12 years.

The 5th – Step to Success is to Keep New Ideas.

Ideas cause you to be a dreamer. They help you to evaluate your dreams and they help you to understand your dreams because without understanding them; you will always have confusion in your life. Ideas help you to study and research your dreams because your dreams are your Ideas and your blueprint in life for what you are about to build and become. You must become your dreams and once you become your dreams you can live your dreams. Once you are living your dreams you are no longer just a dreamer but your dreams have become your reality and you have become the real estate, as well as the evidence and product of what you have just built and discovered.

Things to remember while reaching for success.

While others may have called your ideas or dreams a mistake they have now become your success. Keep new ideas and keep dreaming because idea's need to be innovated, inspired, on the cutting edge and always rejuvenated. Having ideas is important to a being a dreamer, but becoming the interpreter and having the ability to define your dreams and ideas is equally important.

The 6th – Step to Success is Succession Planning

Succession Planning means improving and becoming better at what it is you began from the beginning. Succession planning is the process for identifying and developing your strategy and process stages for your structure. It also deals with the cost and time that you're willing to put in to create and have success because nobody can give you success, you must earn and create success for yourself. In succession planning, you're planning for your success. So, never chase success, run after success, lose your identity or your assignment; because you are hungry for success.

Deuteronomy 28:2 NKJV
2 And all these blessings shall come upon you and overtake you, because you obey the voice of the Lord your God.

This simply means when you're following the steps that make up success; you don't have to find success, success will find you and overtake you. Stay in your place! The Bible says in Genesis chapter one, God Himself was a strategist and a planner of succession planning and he developed creation.

Genesis 1:5 NKJV
5 God called the light Day, and the darkness He called Night. So the evening and the morning were the first day.

Genesis 1:8 NKJV
8 And God called the firmament Heaven. So the evening and the morning were the second day.

Genesis 1:13 NKJV
13 So the evening and the morning were the third day.

Genesis 1:19 NKJV
19 So the evening and the morning were the fourth day.

Genesis 1:23 NKJV
23 So the evening and the morning were the fifth day.

Genesis 1:31 NKJV
31 Then God saw everything that He had made, and indeed it was very good. So the evening and the morning were the sixth day.

This simply means God was a succession planner of each day. He planned what would be manifested and brought things forward each day because God was a master builder and strategist.

The 7th – Step to Success is Serve and a be a Servant

The greatest level to success is the heart and ability to serve, having a heart of sacrifice and offering your services; this is what makes one successful at being a servant. This is the administrative gift called "the gift of helps", "the gift of hospitality" and "the gift of giving". It is an administrative gift that creates multiplication of favor and blessings. God gives the resources to supply all the needs of the saints and of people who are less fortunate; to accommodate the servants of God as well as the vessels of God. They are the forerunners of God.

1 Corinthians 12:28 NLT
28 Here are some of the parts God has appointed for the church: first are apostles, second are

prophets, third are teachers, then those who do miracles, those who have the gift of healing, those who can help others, those who have the gift of leadership, those who speak in unknown languages.

Giving empowers one in an extraordinary way to understand or discern the material or financial needs of others and then meet those needs. The more one uses this gift of service, the more God prospers one. So, the person with this gift of service is enabled to give without ever running out. Giving literally means in the Greek, he who provides in giving aid. This gift of service/gift of giving equips one to see the practical needs, the resources and the abilities of others so that their needs are met.

2 Corinthians 9:12-13 NKJV
12 For the administration of this service not only supplies the needs of the saints, (God Becomes Your Personal Banker) but also is abounding through many thanksgivings to God.

13 while, through the proof of this ministry, they glorify God for the obedience of your confession to the gospel of Christ, and for your liberal sharing with them and all men.

2 Corinthians 9:10-13 ERV

10 God is the one who gives seed to those who plant, and he gives bread for food. And God will give you spiritual seed and make that seed grow. He will produce a great harvest from your goodness. 11. God will make you rich in every way so that you can always give freely. And your giving through us will make people give thanks to God. 12 The Service you are offering Helps God's people with their needs, but that is not all it does. It is also bringing more and more thanks to God. 13 This Service is a proof of your faith, and people will praise God because of it. They will praise God that you freely share what you have with them and with all people. They will praise him to see you following the Good News about Christ that you openly accepted. They will praise God because you freely share with them and with all people.

Mark 10:45 NIV

45 For even the Son of Man did not come to be served, but to serve, and to give his life as a ransom for many.

Luke 22:26-27 GW

26 But you're not going to be that way! Rather, the greatest among you must be like the youngest, and your leader must be like a servant. 27 Who's the greatest, the person who sits at the table or the servant? Isn't it really the person who sits at the table? But I'm among you as a servant.

The 8th - Step to Success is Patience.

Patience means the ability to endure, to complete and to finish. It is the ability, the gift and favor from God to endure until the end. Patience helps you outlast your enemy, your problem and your storms.

Patience is a virtue which means waiting without complaint. The word virtue means good behavior, good quality, righteousness, Integrity, honor, decency, goodness, power and strength.
When you hear the phrase 'patience is a virtue,' this phrase means patience has the ability to wait for something or someone without being angry, upset or excessively frustrated.

Luke 8:46-47 KJV
46 And Jesus said, Somebody hath touched me: for I perceive that Virtue is gone out of me. 47 And when the woman saw that she was not hid, she came trembling, and falling down before him,

she declared unto him before all the people for what cause she had touched him, and how she was healed immediately.

Patience is the Virtue that makes up all 8 Steps of Success.

- You have to have patience to find and discover your passion.

- You need patience to work when you don't feel like working. When it's not in you to work, when you're ready to stop, quit and give up it takes patience to trust God to Work It Out!

- It takes patience to stay focused when everything around you is trying to become a distraction and bring you down.

- It takes patience to be able to push yourself and encourage yourself when you're at the point of giving up.

- It takes patience when your ideas and your dreams are not coming to pass as fast as you'd like them to come.

- It takes patience to understand succession planning, developing and being motivated; when at the same time discouragement has brought you negativity, rejection, criticism. Like Nehemiah and the people of God that are working along with him; you must continue to stay on the wall while working your assignment as well as keep the mind to work while the enemy is coming to discourage and frustrate your purpose.

- It takes patience to serve and to be a good servant. The more you try to help people, do for people, be there for people and bless people; the more they are ungrateful, and unappreciative and will take you for granted. The more you try to help people and serve people the more they expect from you; they use you and abuse you. You must be patient and remember the Word of God according to...

Matthew 5:44 NKJV
44 But I say to you, love your enemies, bless those who curse you, do good to those who hate you, and pray for those who spitefully use you and persecute you.

When you look throughout the old and new testament and find someone that signifies patience they had virtue, they had integrity, they endured and they outlasted their storm as well as their problems. There was no one greater than Job. God himself testified to Satan that Job was a man of integrity, a man of good report and no matter what he would go through; he would trust God!

Job lost all his property, his cattle, his children were killed, sickness came over his body, he lost his health, his wife encouraged him out of her own hurt and frustration to curse God and die.

Job 2:9 NLT
9 His wife said to him, "Are you still trying to maintain your integrity? Curse God and die."

The book of Job starts off by talking about Job's value, wealth and success. He had 7,000 sheep, 3,000 camels, 500 yoke of oxen and 500 female donkeys. The Bible points out that Job was the richest man in the land of Uz, and he feared and reverenced God. He was a man of integrity, honesty, good character and he was a righteous man. Job was a virtuous Man which these are all the definitions for the word patience. The Bible says God had called a court summit with the DA which is Satan the prosecutor on the indictment and accusation that Satan had brought up against Job. God asked Satan where are you coming from? Satan's response was here and there, up and down your earth seeking whom I can find fault with and bring charges on. God asked Satan have you considered my servant Job? The first thing we understand about Job is the reason he's so successful and rich is because he was a servant, the 7th step of success and he knew how to give his service in the kingdom for God for mankind. Then we learn that God, testifies on Job's behalf. He says to Satan, Job is a man of integrity, honesty, good character, power, and strength, a virtuous man and a man of endurance. This simply meant that Job was a man of patience. Satan appealed to God, how is Job so successful and considered by You a man of virtue, a man of endurance, integrity, honesty, good character, power, and strength? God testifying on Job's behalf meant that he was successful because he knew how to live his life being patient.

Satan's response back to God was how can you testify on Job's behalf that he is patient and has success; that you have given him; when he hasn't been through anything? Satan said; allow me to attack his integrity, honesty, good character, power, strength, and his endurance. Allow me to attack his patience and let's watch how successful he'll be. Once God gave Satan permission to attack Job's success; Satan attacked his success by seeing how patient Job would be.

Satan's attack on Job's Success

Satan attacked 7 things of Job's success that dealt with Job's patience. The first thing he attacked was Job's finances. Second, was his property. Third, was Job's Family. The fourth attack was on Job's health. The fifth attack was on his marriage and the sixth attack was on his friendships. The seventh attack was on Job's Integrity which was his honesty, good character, power, strength, ability to be a virtuous man and his ability to endure. This was an attack on Job's patience.

Once your money has been attacked, your property (car, house, etc.), family, health, marriage and friendship; all you have to hold onto is your integrity, honesty and good character. In other words all you have left is your name and your trust and faith that God will see you through. Stay patient, trust, wait and believe that God will keep you and see you through because they that wait upon the Lord, He will renew their strength.

God testified to Satan about Job being a man of integrity/patience and , to paraphrase; He said no matter how you attack Job he will patiently trust Me and believe in Me even though you have attacked and taken his success, property, finance, marriage, and friendships. His integrity and his patience will cause him to believe that out of all his appointed time to wait patiently until his change come!

What made Job so successful was that he was a man of patience. A man that had gone through tribulation, persecution, the loss of his family, the loss of his houses, land, cattle, servants and his health and he still had patience.

Job 1:21 AMP
21 And said, "Naked (without possessions) came I [into this world] from my mother's womb, and naked shall I return there. The Lord gave and the Lord has taken away; blessed be the name of the Lord."

Job 14:14 KJV
14 If a man die, shall he live again? all the days of my appointed time will wait till my change come.

Patience is a gift from God that gives you the ability to endure and outlast all that you're going through. From Job chapters 1 and 2, he had lost everything but in Job chapter 42, patience helped him to outlast everything he had lost. Job chapter 42, says he got double for his trouble because the greatest level to success is not to focus on the C.R.A.P. you're going through or the C.R.A.P. you're experiencing but to know real success deals with what doesn't kill you but makes you stronger and better! Job got double for his trouble because he had patience to outlast his storms, trials, tribulations, persecution, criticism, rejection, adversary (Satan) and because he stayed persistent and patient. Job's patience helped him outlast and endure all the C.R.A.P. that Satan attacked him with. When you successfully complete the 8th - Step for Success, patience, you will complete final step that will help you to complete the other 7 steps.

You'll never be successful in your life if you do not have patience that produces integrity, honesty, a good attitude with the characteristics that help you to walk in excellence and endurance. You'll never be successful in life if you don't outlast whatever comes at you in life. Things will come to steal, kill and destroy but you have to have patience. You must believe and trust with all patience that Christ has come that you may have life and that you can have it more abundantly. In Job chapter 42, God gave Job more abundantly. He got double for His trouble because of his patience.

Chapter 7

Developing & Growing Success

Topic Scripture: Genesis 26:1 says, there was a double famine in that ground where Isaac lived. In Genesis 26:2, the Lord appeared unto Isaac and told him, do not go back to Egypt but be obedient unto his instructions. In Genesis 26:12, it says, out of obedience Isaac sowed seeds into that ground during a double famine and in that same year he received 100 times more than he sowed seeds. Don't miss a God moment because you keep having a you moment that causes you instead of growing in success and reaping success; it causes you to keep reaping failure because you're allowing what is called seeds of discord to be sowed into your life. Seeds of discord are a lack of harmony, confusion, disagreement, conflict, strife, hostility, argument, division, and hatred. Sowing seeds of discord are what caused Isaac and many other believers to keep missing their seasons of success as well as their growth from success.

Matthew 13:24, Jesus tells a parable about a farmer that sowed good seeds in the ground of his season that after he had sown the good seeds, the enemy came and sowed seeds of discord or tare in the same season and in the same ground and when his disciples came and asked him why is it that their harvest or season is not growing in success? Jesus said because while you were sleeping the enemy came and sowed seeds of discord to bring confusion, failure, strife, and hatred into your season. This is what has happened in Genesis 26, every time Isaac sowed seed as well as unstopped or dug up wells the enemy came and sowed seeds of discord called envy, strife, jealousy and hatred but Isaac kept being persistent. He was persuaded that not only would he be successful but he would develop and grow in success.

Genesis 26:12, Isaac sowed seeds into the ground in that environment and reaped in the same year 100 times more than he sowed seed. The secret to Isaac's success and what had helped him to develop and grow success was that he was able to change the culture of the ground by understanding the identity of the seed. Genesis 26 says, the ground was barren and was unproductive, unfruitful and was not yielding fruit, harvest or increase, but when Isaac sowed seed into the ground his seed changed the culture of the ground. Culture means the deposit of knowledge, experience, beliefs, values, attitudes, religion, the notion of time, behavior, and the products with human works and thoughts that develop and bring forth the totality of a socially transmitted behavior pattern that will either develop success or failure. Our culture represents our environment and our surroundings. So, what is the environment like in your home, church, job, community and city? Because your environment will try to dictate your culture; the way you think, how you live and how you believe. If you do not change the culture of your thinking you cannot change how you live and believe in your home, church, job, or anywhere else. You will always create a hostile environment to live in, to praise God in and to work in.

Culture deals with **"Change the Way You Think and You Will Change the Way You Live"** When Isaac sowed into the famine of the ground his seed changed the culture and environment of the ground by impregnating a ground that was barren, not useful, unproductive and impotent. The seed caused the ground to become pregnant because the ground is the womb and the incubator and it needs a seed to become pregnant. The seed is the DNA; which is the genes or living organism that produces genetic evidence. The seed gives the ground life by changing its culture. The ground won't work without a seed. The ground can't become pregnant without a seed and the ground won't produce a harvest without a seed.

A woman can't become pregnant without a seed. If you want to bring forth new life, you have to have a seed to change the culture of the ground! When Isaac sowed his seed in that season his seed changed the culture and environment in the ground by impregnating it immediately. When a seed is deposited into the ground, the ground changes its culture. It gains knowledge, beliefs, and values. The ground took on a new attitude and a new behavior. The ground that was failing in its season began to become successful because of the seed. In order to understand developing the growth of success we must change our thinking and the mindset of what we've been taught all of our lives. In order to grow successfully we have to shift our thinking from goal consciousness to growth consciousness because you can set all the goals you want for yourself in life and you can change; but still not grow. It is possible to change without growing but it's impossible to grow without changing.

Goal Consciousness vs. Growth Consciousness

GOAL CONSCIOUSNESS	GROWTH CONSCIOUSNESS
1. Goal Consciousness teaches us to focus on a destination.	1. Growth Consciousness teaches us to focus on a journey.
2. Goal Consciousness motivates you and others.	2. Growth Consciousness matures you and others.
3. Goal Consciousness is Seasonal.	3. Growth Consciousness is lifelong. It's a lifetime.
4. Goal Consciousness challenges you.	4. Growth Consciousness changes you.
5. Goal Consciousness stops when the Goal is reached.	5. Growth Consciousness keeps you GROWING beyond the Goal.

The key to making the right changes; that will allow us to grow; is understanding the difference between problems and challenges. Problems you can change, solve or correct. Challenges which deal with the facts of life you typically cannot change.

The facts of life such as where and when you were born cannot be changed. You cannot change who your parents are, you cannot change your race, or your DNA. These are the facts of life that may challenge you because you don't like them but you cannot change them, but you can change your attitude about them.

Isaac's problem changed in the famine of his debt; where he lived and how he lived, his problem changed when he sowed his seed into the ground. His seed canceled the debt of brokenness on his life. His seed also changed the culture of the ground and caused the ground to take on a new attitude and mindset which caused a broken ground that once; only produced poverty seasons; to change the ground into a culture that began to produce prosperity because "**When You Change the Way You Think You Change the Way You Live**". (**Word of Deliverance - Church Motto**)

So always understand your thinking always deals with a culture of thinking, a mentality or a mindset. You don't have a money problem you have a thinking problem.

Ecclesiastes 10:19b
But money solves a lot of problems.

Money will always be the answer to your problems. If you don't have a money problem you have a thinking problem. The Bible says money is the answer to all things. It does not say money is the problem but rather money is the answer. So, when you quit looking at money you don't have as your problem, and instead see the money that you do have; you'll solve your problem and correct your problem like Isaac did.

Isaac's 4 Processes for Developing and Growing Success.

The 1st - Process is called the place of Gerar.
Gerar means a place of circles or cycles; the place of my complacency, being average and mediocre. Gerar wasn't the well that Isaac dug up first. It was the place where Isaac lived. Before, we can dig up our old wells and dig new wells, we first have to cultivate our grounds and change the culture of how we live because until you change how you live, you will always struggle where you live.

Genesis 26:19-20 ERV
19 Isaac's servants also dug a well near the little river and found fresh water. 20 But the men who herded sheep in the Valley of Gerar argued with Isaac's servants. They said, "This water is ours." So Isaac named that well Esek. He gave it that

name because it was the place where they had argued with him.

The 2nd - Process is called the place of Esek.
This simply means a place of contention. A place of confusion, strife, hostility and jealousy. Another level or process for developing growth called success is when you can be in a hostile environment where people sow seeds of discord; to stop up your success or blessings; while at the same time becoming envious and jealous of you. While you're still able to be blessed; because you're not allowing people who are stagnated and full of jealousy to hinder you from being blessed. You understand you have been given a ground and an opportunity to sow your seed to change the culture of your ground. Your enemies are stagnated and jealous of you when they had the same opportunity to sow their seed and to change the culture of how they live but they would rather be jealous of you and your success than to become successful themselves.

The 3rd – Process is called the place of Sitnah.
This simply means anger, bitterness and hatred.

Genesis 26:21 ERV

21 Then Isaac's servants dug another well. But there was an argument over this well too. So Isaac named that well Sitnah.

Sitnah is a place of violence and fighting. It represents you beginning to develop the 3rd level of growth for your success. When you can be in an environment where your enemy is not only angry or bitter with you but to the point that they have become violent and they want to fight you over what's yours. They would rather fight you over what's yours than fight for what is theirs.

The 4th - Process is called the place of Rehoboth.

Genesis 26:22 ERV

22 Isaac moved from there and dug another well. No one came to argue about this well. So Isaac named it Rehoboth. He said, "Now the Lord has found a place for us. We will grow and be successful in this place."

Rehoboth means the place of my breakthrough, my over flow, my fruitfulness, my abundance, my increase and a place called more than enough; where God makes more room for me.

When you have reached this 4th process of development of growth for your success you will have come to a place where you have outgrown the place of Gerar as well as the people and the spirit of familiarity. Here is where you stop going through your cycles, circles and complacency. Rehoboth is where you no longer live an average or mediocre life. Here you are no longer distracted or stagnated about what people think about you, say about you or how they feel about you.

There are 4 places you have outgrown.

The 1st - place you would have outgrown is Gerar; the place of complacency, average, mediocre and uncertainty. You would have outgrown your cycles that have taken you in circles called your failure.

The 2nd - place you would have outgrown is Esek; the place of envy, strife, jealousy as well as confusion that tried to hold you hostage in a hostile environment.

The 3rd - place you would have outgrown is Sitnah; the place where those that hate you, despitefully use you, deliberately try to pick a fight with you, try to expose your character and where they try to undermine and sabotage your success.

Finally, when you reach the 4th process of your development of growth for success you have maximized your complete capacity called <u>Rehoboth</u>; where you have not only moved pass your enemy, overlooked your enemy, out classed your enemy, out planned your enemy and have more integrity than your enemy. You have also outgrown your enemy and that's why they're still fighting and hating you over the minor! You have graduated to the major! You no longer major in the minor, you major in the major and that's why they hate you for your success because success looks good on you!

Wells represent biblical and symbolical blessings, resource, life, wealth and success but you have to learn how to dig up wells as well as unstop wells. In order to receive your resources, your blessings, your wealth and your success you have to unstop some wells. Before Isaac unstopped the old wells and dug new wells he first had to cultivate the ground at Gerar because developing the growth of success starts in sowing.

1 Corinthians 3:7 GWT
7 So neither the one who plants nor the one who waters is important because only God makes it grow.

There's a sowing process, and a watering process but God brings forth the growing process, because one plant, one waters but God brings forth the growth!

3 Types of Wells

The 1st is old wells which represent foundation, truth, promises and the Word of God. (The Book of Ezra & Nehemiah)

The 2nd is new wells which represent structure and fresh water. This simply means new revelation, new resource, new innovation, new ideas and new reformation.

The 3rd is generational wells or Rehoboth; which represent a new generation, a new source of income, increasing inheritance, a new culture, freedom, peace, a new millennium and a generational blessing!

PSALMS 30:5b NKJV
35 weeping may endure for a night, but joy cometh in the morning.

God is about to make many who are reading these instructions and who will be obedient to this Word; cause what has hurt you, what has caused you pain, and what has caused you trouble and tears to be turned into laughter!

Chapter 8

<u>MAINTAINING SUCCESS</u>

Definition of maintaining means the act of continuing to retain something at a certain rate. This means to affirm, to keep up, to continue to assert. It implies confidence, to vindicate, and to validate. It means to support a style of living. The Latin word for maintaining means to protect against the liability; to practice habitually and to carry on.

<u>Maintaining (vs.) Maintenance</u>

Maintaining Success is when you work on it or when you build it up. Maintenance is when you keep working on fixing and repairing it. It's becomes an ongoing process that has no completion because you put more in it than you can get out of it.

Too many marriages, relationships and financial problems, have been getting maintenance, but they have not been maintained. We have been paying too much maintenance and its costing us too much to keep paying on something that keeps tearing up or falling apart. This is what's called high maintenance repair, which means needing a lot of work to keep it up, but what you discover in the end is that it's only a liability. In order to maintain success you have to be able to deal with the attacks and fallouts that try to get you to quit; stop; and to even give up and go back to your life as usual. However, true success to in life in any capacity requires that you stay innovative and on the cutting edge. You also, need to keep your passion fueled with fire.

There is only one major thing that can kill your success and stop you from being innovative. It's called "refusing to change".

Just a decade ago, Blockbuster was ruled the number one movie and rental business in the nation. They had 50 million dollars in annual cash flow and was valued at 4.8 billion dollars. Yet, Blockbuster soon filed for bankruptcy because there was a newer company called Netflix gaining leadership in the industry. In September 2010, Blockbuster posted 1.1 billion dollars in revenue losses with the company's value of just 24 million dollars.

Netflix gained 6 million subscribers by running a well-executed operation and was streaming movies online. In 2011, Netflix's net income was 226 million dollars and they were valued at a billion dollars. The crazy thing is Netflix was offered to Blockbuster for 50 million dollars in the year 2000; however,

Blockbuster declined the offer. Failing to prepare and respond to change led Blockbuster to bankruptcy.

Netflix saw change coming and used it to become one of the leading on-demand internet video companies in the world. Blockbuster did not see Netflix coming in the rear view mirror and they failed to maintain success. So, now the number one business in the world that deals with video is no longer in business because it failed to not only make adjustments but to maintain their success and stay innovative.

How many of us have started out successfully in whatever adventure we set out to do because we know how to start, but we don't know how to finish? There is no such place when developing and growing success that does not bring attacks, competitiveness, competition, controversy and deception along with someone who is trying to maintain success. In order to be successful at maintaining success, we must understand the attacks that come against anyone that's trying to build success. Nehemiah went through several attacks while he was trying to build and maintain success.

Building and Maintaining Success

Nehemiah in the beginning processes of maintaining success discovered that the walls and the city of Jerusalem had been burned down and destroyed. When he was given that message, this was the beginning process for Nehemiah's success; because it was then that he found his passion.

- In the book of Nehemiah; we discover that Nehemiah finds his passion. You'll always know your passion and assignment; because anytime you witness or hear about anyone that is hurting and it's troubling; immediately it impacts your life. Their hurt, their trouble and what they're going through with their problems becomes your problem. Because what they cannot solve, your passion helps solve!

- Nehemiah takes on the burden and the responsibility of the assignment to do the "work" that requires him to go back to Jerusalem to help build the wall and bring restoration and a cultural change to the city.

- Nehemiah had to understand as a cupbearer, being assigned to the King, how to stay focused, be multi-talented, be multi-purposed and at the same time, be a cupbearer, and a strategic planner, that has taken on a new assignment of reformation as well as proclamation.

- Nehemiah was able to follow as a follower and lead as a leader. He submitted to the king, as a cupbearer but at the same time he was able to step out as a leader and lead the people with the burden of the assignment that he had been given.

- Pushing yourself and learning how to be persistent. Nehemiah pushed himself and was fully persuaded to come up with a strategic strategy that he brought before the king.

- Nehemiah was a man that kept new ideas, as well as being Innovative and being strategic. When the king challenged Nehemiah while his countenance was down before him, Nehemiah began to share his passion as well as his ideas.

- Nehemiah knew how to do succession planning, as well as maintain success. He was able to correspond and engineer as a master architect as well as a constructor in the re-building and he was able to tell the king how long it would take

Nehemiah was multi-gifted with multi-purpose and he knew how to wear multiple hats. He was able to tell the king exactly how many days it would take to rebuild the walls, (52 days), how much money it would take to build the walls, and who (manpower) it would take to re-build the walls. He knew who the workers would be as well as the adversaries that would come against them. Nehemiah also knew the enemies that were enemies against them and one another, would become allies and join forces to come against something or someone that they had as an enemy in common. That's just to say that for as much as they hated one another, they hated you more.

When you are doing something towards maintaining success, you have got to know your ABC's and what it will take from beginning to end. When people of influence ask you the cost, the time and procedures, you must give them A-Z. When you are finished and have completed the assignment, you can look back and say now I know my ABC's tell me now what you think of me.

3 Processes of Maintaining Success
- 1st - Process for maintaining success deals with how to identify and evaluate your greatest needs and where to start the work of your assignment.

Nehemiah 2:1-15: Nehemiah went down to Jerusalem at night and identified, evaluated and assessed the damage of the walls, the gates and the doors. Nehemiah assessed where he needed to get started just as you must always be able to assess your assignment, the cost to repair the damages and to see if this is something you can maintain or something you'll have to maintenance before you even get started.

- 2nd - Process is identifying your partners that will be networking or connecting with you. The Bible says, Nehemiah assessed and identified the damage and he began to call the leaders, the officials and the heads of the families to partner with him. (Nehemiah 2:16-20)

Luke 19 talks about Jesus connecting with a partner called Zacchaeus. We find out when you're starting to do something of great importance, you have to find people that will become investing partners; they will become the contributing partners and they will help market the partnership. You have to identify the employer's and the employee's.

- 3rd - Process is maintaining partnerships that deals with assigning people to their greatest strengths, assets, as well as to their passion. Also, to position and place them where they can succeed without failing; where they have the most to gain and the least to lose.

Never position anyone into a position or place of authority or a place of power and he or she has nothing to lose. Keep partners in your life that are not there to tolerate you but that are assigned to celebrate you. Make sure the people that you allow in your life, especially in this season, and the season to come are people that will not compete with you, but will complete you. People that compete against you will only tolerate your existence. People that complete you will celebrate you in any and every season.

Maintaining success means you have to be multi-talented, multi-purposed and multi-gifted. Nehemiah had to be able to identify every area of his plan and what would be needed to work the plan. He instructed the people that with one hand they would have tools to build, with the other hand they would have weapons for war, and below the walls they had trumpeters that brought forth praise and worship. When planning and maintaining success everyone has to know their assignments. You have to know when to build with the tools you've been given and how to work with the weapons that have been placed in your hands to defend the work against any attack. The trumpets that have been placed in your hands are to praise the work that you are doing and to completely give glory back to God. Because being multi-talented, multi- purposed and multi-gifted teaches us how to build, how to defend and how to praise at the same time and this they did for 24 hours a day. They had eight hours for work eight hours to defend and protect the work; and eight hours for praise and worship. This is how they balanced their life maintaining success daily.

Luke 5, talks about the disciples trying to catch fish all night and failed. The disciples were given an assignment by Jesus, as they allowed Jesus to come on their boat. After Jesus finished ministering to the multitude, He told His new partners to launch out to the deep and catch an abundance of fish. The Bible says, after they overcame the failure of last night, from weeping, they were able to reap the joy that came in the new morning. The Bible says, they caught so many fish that they had to signal for their partners to come, help catch and celebrate their abundance of fish.

These scriptures tell us 4 things about success:

- 1st - It tells us that they called for their partners, This is an indication to us that you have got to have people in your life that don't mind networking or partnering with you to have success.

- 2nd - They called on their partner's to help them catch their success.

- 3rd - You have got to have people in your life to

help you share the success. If we agree to catch it; we ought to be able to share it.

- 4th - You must have partners in your life that will help you celebrate your success.

Chapter 9
The Attack on Success

Success takes time to build and maintain and it always comes with conflict and haters. Nehemiah had developed his plan for success and he had given it to the king, but he understood the cost of his assignment and that it would not come without opposition and attack to their success.

The 1st - Attack by the enemy was to Humiliate what they had started doing (Nehemiah 4:3).

When you begin to do something, especially something of significance, there comes great obstacles. The enemy, who knows of your past and present life battles, your failures and your strengths, comes to distract and humiliate you. He comes to make what you have done this far in your life look less than value or average. He understands who you are in this new season of your life and that's why he's laughing and trying to humiliate you and what you are doing in this season. The enemy's reason for laughing and trying to humiliate you is to cause you to feel belittled and to shame you so he can convince you that what you are doing is less than nothing and its serving no purpose for accomplishment. So, what he's really saying to you is quit, give up and stop because you're embarrassing yourself.

Nehemiah 4:3 GW
3 Tobiah the Ammonite, who was beside Sanballat, said, "Even a fox would make their stone wall collapse if it walked on top of what they're building!"

The 2nd – Attack Intimidates:

Nehemiah 4:14-23, is when the enemy brings intimidation. Intimidation means to create a fear factor. When the enemy can't humiliate you, he then tries to intimidate you and then manipulate you. The enemy tries through fear factors to get you to stop, quit or give up what God has assigned you to do. When the attacks come it is an indication that your enemy is more threatened by you than you are of him. The Bible says, the enemies of Nehemiah, as well as Jerusalem, started off by laughing and humiliating the work that Nehemiah and the workers were doing. They were saying things like, 'you have taken burnt and cheap bricks and people that are broken and living in poverty to a city that has been destroyed or burnt down for over 70 years.' A place that has been in ruins for 70 years and is beyond salvaging and you think that you can re-do, restore and re-build. But, when the enemy saw that he couldn't humiliate you into stopping he thought he could manipulate you into quitting. Now that he cannot manipulate you into quitting, he's trying to intimidate you to make you give up. Any time the enemy goes this far out of the way to get you to give up or quit, he is the one intimidated because he sees something you cannot completely see yourself.

3rd - Attack: Confusion and discouragement by the enemy to frustrate your purpose and assignment. (Nehemiah 4 and Ezra 4)

Confusion and discouragement cause you to become mentally fatigued and burned out. They cause you to second guess yourself and everyone else. The enemy will not only try to bring confusion and discouragement but his ultimate plan is to cause people to turn on one another, to begin to look at one another differently, to judge one another differently, talk to one another differently and to treat one another differently in the name of confusion, discouragement and division. Confusion will cause a united house to become a divided house, a united people to become a divided people and it will cause one vision to become division, all because the enemy knows a house that is divided against itself cannot stand and he does not want us to stand united.

So, this attack of confusion allows the enemy to no longer have to fight you from the outside in; but he knows that when people are discouraged and confused and at a place of division he can attack from the inside out. Confusion, and discouragement gave the enemy the weapons he needed to fight you from the inside out. The inside is where he has always caused confusion. From the time of Cain and Abel, through Abraham and Lot, Jacob and Esau, David (1 Samuel 30) and the men that turned on him and talked about killing him, to the time of Jesus and His disciple Judas. He knows that he can only destroy an assignment that God has given His people from the inside out not the outside in. Once Satan realizes his weapons are limited and he has tried humiliation, intimidation, manipulation, confusion, distraction and discouragement he looks to bring about compromise. Compromise is his final attack against Nehemiah and the workers. He wants them to negotiate like the television show called "Let's Make a Deal" because his other tactics are not getting the expected results. So now he comes to you while you're on the wall working. Nehemiah 6:2, talks about how the enemy came while the workers were on the wall completing the work with Nehemiah overseeing.

Boldly, the enemy is now trying to stop you from working your assignment and to get you to come down off the wall and meet him at his meeting place called Ono.

Many of you fail to recognize, even in this season and time called "May-Day", why you are in trouble and distress. The enemy is taking advantage of your vulnerabilities and fragilities and he's trying to negotiate with you to get you to come down off the wall, to give up, quit and to come down and meet him. He understands that if you quit now or if you come down now, everything you sacrificed, everything you have invested in, and everything you have ever believed in, will be lost; because Ono means a place where I gave up, the place of my demise , the place where I stopped, the place where I quit, and the place of my failure.

It's time for us to tell the enemy and the devil that has tried to negotiate with you......ONO! I can't come down and I can't turn around. Tell the devil ONO, I can't give up and I can't meet you at the place called ONO!

Matthew 27:42, the Bible says the enemy tried to do the same thing to Jesus while He was on the Cross. They laughed at Him, and they tried to humiliate Him,

Jesus kept on praying and interceding. Finally, when they saw He was who He said He was, they told Jesus to come down off the Cross. They were simply saying to Jesus, quit, give up, stop, end this, and don't finish this; however, Jesus refused to come down! Jesus refused to quit. He refused to go to that place called ONO, when He was promised a place called eternity, back in Heaven sitting on the right side of His Father.

You have to say to yourself, I know the work that God has given me to do and this is why I refuse to settle and come down from my assignment. I refuse to settle for Hell; when God has promised me Heaven. ONO, I won't give up, ONO, I won't quit, ONO, I won't stop and like Jesus, ONO, I won't come down. And like the ones who worked with Nehemiah and were on the wall and were doing a great work. We refuse to come down and go to a place called ONO!

Chapter 10

<u>MANAGING CONFLICT</u>

In order to Maintain Success you have to learn how to manage Conflict. The word conflict means struggle, problem, disagreement, battle, friction, confusion, altercation, argument and fighting. It also, means to come into collision or disagreement; to be contradictory or in opposition or to have discord. It means to run interference that causes illegal procedures.

You can't maintain success if you don't know how to manage conflict. Managing conflict deals with understanding and managing attacks, controversy and confusion. It's just as much of the assignment as success is part of the process. Without identifying conflict and understanding how to manage the conflict of ongoing attacks there will be no success.

It's difficult, if not impossible; to think of a relationship of any type that does not encounter disagreements at one time or another. Unless relationships can withstand the stress of conflicts and those in them; manage them productively, they are unlikely to endure because a series of conflicts; as well as attacks bring about an abundance of exposure.

If you're the one managing conflict this means you're the manager or supervisor over it. Therefore you're in power and control of what is happening at all times. For example; if you are the supervisor and the employer of conflict, which simply means you don't work for conflict or confusion; but conflict and confusion work for you. When conflict and confusion don't want to cooperate by the authority that you have over them; you have a right to fire conflict and confusion and hire something else called peace, fulfillment, endurance and faithfulness.

What is Conflict?

Conflict is a disagreement between two or more parties, individuals, groups; it is division or separation between any type of relationship.

What are the main sources of conflict?

Conflict doesn't just magically appear out of thin air. It has various causes but most can be attributed to two reasons.

- Communication Problems
- Personal Indifferences

Managing the Conflict

Communication Problems

Communication problems are disagreements that frequently arise from misinterpreting, misunderstandings, poor listening, bad and noisy frequency in the communication channels such as; screaming at one another, yelling at one another, fussing at one another, and yes even cursing one another.

People are often quick to assume that most conflicts are caused by lack of communication. In reality, there is usually plenty of communication during a conflict. The mistake many people make is when they think good communication is only right when other people agree with what they are saying or when other people agree with only their views. Assuming that if others don't except your position or what you are saying does not indicate that there is a communication problem. The reality is that the conflict based on poor communication is quiet often determined to be a disagreement caused by factors such as misunderstandings, different value systems and different mindsets.

Personal Indifferences

Personal Indifferences evolves out of individuals, personal value systems and poor chemistry between some people makes it hard for them to work together. Factors such as cultural backgrounds, education, experience and training makes each individual into a unique personality with a particular set of values and behavioral style. The result is that people may be perceived by others as abrasive, untrustworthy, or strange by individuals with different backgrounds and belief systems.

The conflict that is created by these types of personal indifferences is sometimes based upon stereotypes; people's prejudice and bias. These conflicts arise because of people's misinterpretation and misunderstanding of your creative concepts and who you are. So, in return the personal indifferences create confusing scenarios.

Managing Conflict - Structural Design Indifferences

Agreeing on how to get from where you are to where you are going. Many times conflict takes place in what is called structural design indifferences that brings forth a new reformation, a new creed or establishing a new order. This takes place in many organizational structures. People have become so accustom to doing things how they have always done them and they don't know things have to change. Like the Blockbuster Structure (vs.) Netflix Structure. It's not that Blockbuster didn't have a structural design but when time changed and they stayed with the same structure. It caused Blockbuster to file bankruptcy; because Blockbuster wasn't open for change. They are no longer in tune or in touch with a world that is revolving as well as evolving. Blockbuster was not open to change, new decisions and the criteria of adjustments. It lost its innovation and above all it lost its ability and focus to grow. Anything that is not willing to change cannot grow and it will die!

Things to do and things not to do when managing conflict.

1st thing to do is called Avoidance (Avoid Unnecessary Conflict).

Avoidance's root word is called avoid. This simply means to keep away from or stop one's self from doing; many times in order to manage conflict. We must quit giving so much of our attention and focus as well as energy to our enemy. The enemy should not have access to your life, know your schedule, your routine and your day better than you do.

In order to understand avoidance you have to learn how to starve your enemy to death by not feeding them, fueling them or empowering them. Because not every conflict requires you; to take a demanding approach. Sometimes avoidance will cause you to withdraw or cancel the conflict; because some conflicts will not be resolved no matter what you do or what you say. Regardless, of how much time and energy you put in it; the best thing you can do as it relates to certain conflicts is to avoid it by unplugging it or by cutting off its power.

The only times you deal with "avoid, avoiding and avoidance" conflicts *is* when the battles have nothing to do with your tomorrow, but has everything to do with your yesterday or your past. You can never win a battle or conflict when it deals with your yesterday so avoid that conflict at all cost! Pick and choose your battles, wisely!

Examples of what Conflicts to Avoid -
Unnecessary Conflicts

1st - Never argue with anyone that chooses to
          disagree with you about who you are.

2nd - Never argue about what you're called to do.

3rd - Never argue about what you're doing.

4th - Never argue with anyone that always reminds you about your past failures because they are still trying to see you as they have always seen you. They struggle with the Spirit of Familiarity and they refuse to let your past go and see you as you really are and for who you are becoming. Jesus was in Nazareth and not only His kinsmen; but the residents of Nazareth could never see Jesus as the Messiah or Savior because of the Spirit of Familiarity. Every time He visited His home town, where He grew up; and would go back to do ministry, they always reminded Him by asking; are you not Joseph and Mary's son? Are you not the son of a carpenter?

2nd thing to do is called Don't Run or Fear Conflict but Embrace it Head On!

Just like there's a time to avoid conflict, there is also a time we must face conflict head on. There are battles that deal with your yesterday and then there are battles that deal with your tomorrow. The battles of your yesterday; that you have moved past; that have refused to allow you to live on and they keep bringing up the past conflicts of your life; avoid them at all cost. But the battles that bring conflict; that you have ignored; you must face them head on because there is a difference between avoiding and ignoring.

Ignore means to disregard intentionally; refuse, not to pay attention to; refuse to take notice or to acknowledge things that need to be taken care of. Avoid means to keep away or stop one's self from doing to keep clear and to prevent or keep something from happening that doesn't need to happen.

The battles that deals with your tomorrow. That you have ignored, not avoided; will always face you going into your future. Because what you refuse to confront today will always confront you tomorrow; because you failed to face that conflict; face to face and head on.

The Bible says in Genesis chapter 32, Jacob ran for over 20 years from his brother Esau because of an ongoing conflict. Esau ran after Jacob for over 20 years and plotted to kill Jacob for stealing his inheritance. The Bible says, God confronted Jacob and told him to no longer run from your brother Esau but confront him, face him head on. Jacob was not only running from Esau but he was also running from his fear, his problems and controversy, because every time Jacob had a problem he quit, gave up, and ran away; but after 20 year's God confronted him.

Genesis 32:24 ERV
24 Jacob was left alone, and a man came and wrestled with him. The man fought with him until the sun came up.

Jacob wrestled with God and confronted his conflict; until he conquered it. He overcame all his fears by telling God, I'm no longer going to run from my problems and conflict but this time I'm going to embrace them. I will not let go until you bless me; and that day Jacob left the presence of God in pain and with a limp but he left with victory! Because he refused not to run from his fears but deal with his conflicts and embrace them head on.

Jacob not only confronts his fears and conflicts that he had with God but he also stopped running and fearing the conflict that he had with his brother Esau. He confronted and embraced a 20 year old struggle head on. But what he failed to understand was, 20 years before confronted him 20 years later because he ran with fear and did not deal with the conflict with his brother Esau. What you don't confront today that will confront you tomorrow.

Genesis 33:4 NLT
4 Then Esau ran to meet him and embraced him,
threw his arms around his neck, and kissed him.
And they both wept.

Jacob confronted Esau his brother by facing him
head on. The Bible said, when they embraced a 20
year old yoke was broken around Esau's neck that
fulfilled a 20 year prophesy spoken to Esau by his
father Isaac.

Genesis 27:38-40 NLT
38 Esau pleaded, "But do you have only one
blessing? Oh my father, bless me, too!" Then
Esau broke down and wept.

39 Finally, his father, Isaac, said to him, "You will
live away from the richness of the earth, and
away from the dew of the heaven above.

40 You will live by your sword, and you will serve
your brother. But when you decide to break free,
you will shake his yoke from your neck."

When Esau embraced Jacob his brother, it freed
Jacob from the conflict that lasted over 20 years.
Too many people choose not to confront or manage
their conflict head on or by embracing it, but because
Jacob did not confront his brother Esau with the

conflict that they had; among themselves. It caused Jacob to lose 20 years of his life. Which simply means within those 20 years of Jacob's life he had entered into new relationships, gotten married, had children, and was raising a family but because he struggled with the conflict with his brother it stagnated him and caused him to go in cycles. Jacob was unable to move forward with his life because he struggled with identity. He wrestled with God until he broke a conflict of cycles that lasted 20 years and God told Jacob after 20 years you are no longer Jacob but you are now Israel. Because you have learned how to manage your conflict even in pain and hurt, you have conquered your fears; and you have confronted what you have refused to deal with; you now know how to manage conflict.

3rd thing to do is called View Conflict as an Opportunity not just an Opposition

Every conflict presents you potential for a tremendous teaching and learning opportunity. Where there is a disagreement; there is an opportunity for potential that gives you room for growth and development.

When you're striving to develop your purpose for success, opposition will always assign itself to attack and bring conflict. But you must understand, you cannot manage success if you don't know how to manage conflict.

Conflict is the teacher of success and success is the student of conflict. Conflict deals with attacks, problems and turmoil as well as series of attacks. Nehemiah before he could complete the building of the walls had to go through a series of attacks and conflicts.

In order to be successful you must be able to manage all the things that will bring you conflict because success is a magnet as well as a coming attraction for conflict. Conflict brings troubles and problems and if you can't manage conflict, you cannot maintain success.

The Apostle Paul talks about conflicts. He said every time he tried to do good or be successful evil was present all around him. It keeps bringing him conflict, trouble and problems that try to get him to stop, quit and give up.

Romans 7:21 ERV

21 So I have learned this rule: When I want to do good, evil is there with me.

Romans 7:21-23 AMP
21 So I find it to be a law (rule of action of my being) that when I want to do what is right and good, evil is ever present with me and I am subject to its insistent demands. 22 For I endorse and delight in the law of God in my inmost self [with my new nature]. 23 But I discern in my bodily members [in the sensitive appetites and wills of the flesh] a different law (rule of action) at war against the law of my mind (my reason) and making me a prisoner to the law of sin that dwells in my bodily organs [in the sensitive appetites and wills of the flesh].

4th thing to do is called Compromise

Compromise means to reach a settlement or to settle a dispute by mutual consent. You must first understand that managing conflict deals with compromise and when we're trying to avoid problems as well as trouble you begin to compromise thinking that it will cause your enemy to back up, to stop or to be at peace with you; but the reality is when you don't manage conflict, compromise creeps in. It causes the problem not to get better but worse.

Too many relationships are built on compromise. Such as right (vs) wrong and you call it reaching an agreement. Too many think the argument, the fussing and the fighting will stop if we compromise; but in reality the problem escalates and we did not solve the problem by compromising; we only delayed the problem. It didn't resolve the problem because compromising causes the situation to become fatal. That's why it is so important that we manage the conflict and not try to compromise with our enemy at any time during negotiation; when it concerns your season and your destiny. Compromising and negotiating with a snake will only lead to you being poisoned and it may bring forth your death. No matter how you want to believe that a snake can change always know that it is the snakes nature to be charming, deceiving, cunning, crafty, deceptive harmful and full of poison. When you compromise with a snake; eventually the snake will bite you. So, don't be mad at the snake; just know it was the nature of the snake to bite you. Never compromise with a snake, when it's not the nature of the snake to change. In Genesis the 3rd chapter, we discovered the mistake Eve made by compromising with a snake.

Genesis 3:1-3, tells us about the nature of the snake that he was cunning, charming, crafty and deadly but Eve still compromised. She allowed the snake to charm her and after he charmed her he tricked her; after he tricked her, he deceived her; after he deceived her, he destroyed her relationship with God and her husband and after he destroyed her relationship; he caused her to lose her life.

Genesis 3:3 says, God told Adam as well as Eve the day you allow the snake to do these things to you; and touch this tree that is forbidden you will surely die. So, when you compromise with a snake the end will always bring what John 10:10, talks about; the snake (the devil) comes not but to do three things; steal, kill and destroy. (Annihilate or Genocide)

5th thing to do is called Turning Conflict in Your Favor! (Turning It Around)

2 Kings 6:14-18 talks, about how the enemy conspired to attack and bring conflict to the Man of God called Elisha. They came to his home and surrounded him with conflict. But the Man of God took the conflict and turned it around in his favor.

He spoke to his servant that was with him and said there are more for us than against us. The servant saw the conflict of being outnumbered by his enemies; but the Man of God said to God, open his eyes that he might see. When the servant's eyes were open; the angels of God surrounded their enemies that plotted and planned to not only bring conflict, but to kill the man of God; but God took the conflict and turned it in his favor!

The Bible says, the Man of God took his hand waved it until the enemies all became blind and lost their vision to see. He took the enemies and led them to their enemy's camp; and instead of killing them; they fed them; because when you learn how to manage your conflict you can turn your conflict into your favor.

When, you read about the three Hebrew boys in Daniel chapter three, they turned their conflict into favor. They went from being thrown into the fiery furnace, to being delivered from the fire to governors over the provinces. They received the highest level of promotion in the providence of the kingdom; because they took their conflict and turned it into their favor.

When we read about Joseph in Genesis chapters 37-42, we discover the conflict of Joseph and how he went from being thrown into the pit, arrested and put into Pharaoh's dungeon on death row, but Joseph was able to take his conflict and turn it into his favor. He told his brothers who had conspired to kill him years later, you meant it for my bad; as well as evil;

but God meant it for my good. Joseph had taken the conflict and turned it into His favor.

Lastly, we close with Jesus who that had been lied on, betrayed, suffered, nailed to the cross, and who had died and was buried, but after three days He took the conflict and turned it into his favor. He snatched the keys from Satan and got the victory over death, hell and the grave and declared all power is in my hand!

Chapter 11

Managing vs. Mismanaging Conflicts

When you look at conflicts (vs.) success; it is much easier dealing with success than conflicts. It is harder to accomplish and find success when you're mismanaging your conflicts. Success is easier to embrace; because it's gentle, peaceful, kind, loving, and favorable and always compensates with blessings and benefits. Conflict is hard, troublesome, and controversial, it brings confusion; it brings drama, hurt, pain, and sickness. Ultimately, conflicts blind your vision and can ultimately rob you of your dreams and destiny if they are not managed successfully.

How you manage conflict successfully will determine how much more success will manage you. The longer you put off conflicts, ignore conflicts and mismanage conflicts the more they build up and become what is called "the pressures of life". This buildup of mismanaged conflict causes many symptoms such as stress, anxiety attacks, unnecessary headaches, high blood pressure, mental fatigue and burn out.

This buildup can cause nervous disorders, anger and tantrums. It causes dysfunctional behavior simply because you are allowing your conflicts to manage you rather; then you manage your conflicts successfully!

The 5 Steps for Managing Conflicts

Step 1 - Anticipate.

You must first take time to obtain information that can lead to conflicts.

Step 2 - Prevent.

You must develop strategies before the conflicts occur.

Step 3 - Identify (Personal vs. Professional)

If the conflict is personal or procedural (professional). This simply means if it's personal it deals with how it affects you from a personal view point or mindset; and has become your distraction. But if it's procedural or professional, this simply means; it's part of the process; that deals with your assignment to help bring you to success. You have to learn how to move quickly to manage it!

Step 4 - Keep it professional

Always remember that all conflicts are designed by the enemy to attack your emotions. So, if you allow conflict to attach itself to you emotionally; you will always handle your problem according to how you feel about something or someone; but if you handle and manage your conflicts according to your assignment. You will always be able to handle something or someone professionally and according to how you've been assigned your purpose as well as your destiny. Always keep it professional when you know the enemy is trying to make it personal. He is trying to attack the "psyche" of your emotions and cause you to become distracted by your assignment.

Step 5 - Resolve.

Once you have determined you can't avoid it, you can't ignore it, you can't look away from it, and you can't walk away from it. You must react, by confronting the conflicts of your crisis before your conflicts confront you. Like Jacob you must embrace it head on; in spite of how much it hurts; in spite the pain you are feeling; you can't let go until you resolve it and it blesses you with success.

- The 1st - thing Nehemiah did, he anticipated where the conflicts would come from before he began building.

- The 2nd - thing Nehemiah did, he prevented conflicts. Nehemiah developed strategies; to keep the enemy out; while the work was going on.

- The 3rd – thing Nehemiah did, he identified who was the threat or enemy that would try to sabotage the work from being accomplished.

- The 4th – thing Nehemiah did, he managed the conflicts of the enemy. He also managed the workers; that would complete the work. From being distracted by the conflict of the enemy.

- The 5th – thing Nehemiah did, he resolved the conflicts before he even started the assignment; by disarming his enemy, implementing, arming and equipping the people he empowered to finish what he started.

2 Types of Conflicts that will determine if you are Managing Conflict or Mismanaging Conflict.

- Type 1 - Reacting; to the conflicts. Reacting deals with how the conflicts have dealt with you

- Type 2 - Pro-acting; to the conflicts. Pro-acting is how you dealt with conflicts.

If you are reacting to the situation or problem that deals with your conflicts then you are mismanaging your conflicts.

If you are pro-acting to your conflicts; this simply means you are managing your conflicts and you are dealing with your problem. You successfully manage what can be a potential or futuristic problem before, it becomes a problem that you can't resolve.

Reacting means your conflicts are managing you. Your conflicts are affecting your emotions, feelings, hurt and pain which causes the conflicts; to activate and reactivate continually.

Conflicts are designed by the enemy to cause you to react out of your emotions. It is the enemy's ultimate plan and strategy to create confusion through conflicts. He wants to bring about distraction and to cause you to emotionally be impacted so much so that you will become distracted in the conflict of your emotions and what you're going through; rather than being caught up in the conflicts; of your assignment and where you're trying to get to This conflict will take you in stages or processes of success. This is why you're experiencing a continuation of unnecessary drama. You keep allowing the same past and present conflicts to cause you to always react the same way. It causes you to keep turning on conflicts that have been turned off by reactivating as well as activating the same problems; over and over again.

Pro-active means to take charge, to take action or to rule by complete authority.

Matthew 11:12 NKJV

12 And from the days of John the Baptist until now the kingdom of heaven suffers violence, and the violent take it by force.

Which simply means by being proactive; you're managing; as well as supervising your conflicts. This again means that conflicts are working for you; and you're not being employed by conflicts.

Which means it's working for your good. When you learn how to be proactive; by taking charge, taking action and taking your conflicts by force. You deactivate your conflicts. That means that by silencing the conflict you are taking away it's voice; Your conflicts do not have a voice to speak or power to do when it concerns your assignments because you will always have the last say, concerning your conflicts. If you manage conflicts successfully; your conflicts should always be your silent partner.

Like Jesus did with the storm in **Mark 4:39 NKJV**

39 Then He arose and rebuked the wind, and said to the sea, "peace, be still!" And the wind ceased and there was a great calm.

Jesus got up from the bottom of the boat; when the enemy had sent a storm and an out of control wind He spoke to the conflict of the storm. Jesus deactivated the conflict; and took force, took action, took charge and told the conflict, you are deactivated; be silent, shut up. He left it without a voice. Until, the conflict moved from a storm and transformed into peace; because Jesus said, peace be still.
When you learn how to manage your conflicts, your conflicts will become your success. But you must be proactive and not like the disciples. They reacted to their storm out of their emotion; that created a fear and it caused their conflicts to manage them.

Chapter 12

Problem Solving & Initiating Change

Hostile Environments & Avoiding Pitfalls by
Being a Problem Solver

Genesis 2:7-9 AMP
**7 Then the Lord God formed man from the dust of
the ground and breathed into his nostrils the
breath or spirit of life, and man became a living
being.**

**8 And the Lord God planted a garden toward the
east, in Eden [delight]; and there He put the man
whom He had formed (framed, constituted).**

**9 And out of the ground the Lord God made to
grow every tree that is pleasant to the sight or to
be desired—good (suitable, pleasant) for food;
the tree of life also in the center of the garden,
and the tree of the knowledge of [the difference
between] good and evil and blessing and
calamity.**

Genesis 2:15-17 AMP
**15 And the Lord God took the man and put him in
the Garden of Eden to tend and guard and keep it.**

16 And the Lord God commanded the man, saying, You may freely eat of every tree of the garden;

17 But of the tree of the knowledge of good and evil and blessing and calamity you shall not eat, for in the day that you eat of it you shall surely die.

Hostile Environments

What is a Hostile Environment? The word Hostile means to be harassed, to be bullied, to be taken advantage of, to place a person in an environment that becomes unbearable, unlivable, and unstable An environment that hinders and stagnates a person's ability to be successful.

Hostile means unfriendly, unkindly, bitter, unsympathetic, malicious, vicious, poisonous, obsessed with trying to destroy someone else's life. Hostile also means uncaring, thoughtless, heartless, hard-hearted, and unforgiving.

Pitfall means unseen danger, traps, hazards, setbacks that comes through the act of conspiracy. Pitfalls are not a coincidence, accident or misfortune.

Pitfalls are a deliberate conspiracy act designed by the enemy to plot your falls or failures, to alter your course of greatness in destiny, by changing the outcome of your dreams into a nightmare.

Problem Solving Strategies for Avoiding Pitfalls
Problem solving is a gift and a skill. A problem solver is someone who doesn't focus on the problem, but focuses on the solution to the problem. If you are not part of the solution then you are part of the problem. If you are planning as an individual to overcome the problems that face and confront you in life; these are the things you must begin to ask yourself. Are you're planning and strategizing how to get the answers to your problems.

Are these some of the problems you are facing?
1st - Relational and Social Problems

2nd - Physical and Medical Problems

3rd - Spiritual Problems (where you have lost the intimacy that you once had with God)

4th - Mental Problems such as stress, depression, and mental lapses

5th - Financial Problems such as paying mortgage and rent, car payment, home owner or auto insurance, utilities and etc.

6th - Are you confronting your problem, or is your problem confronting you?

7 Steps to Becoming a Problem Solver

- 1st – Define and Identify the Problem

- 2nd– Determine the Root Cause of the Problem
- 3rd – Eliminate the Problem

- 4th – Develop and Select Option Solution

- 5th – Initiate Change

- 6th – Implement the Solution for Change

- 7th – Evaluate the Outcome

Define and identify the problem deals with decision making. You must first discover or ask yourself these questions.

- What or who has convinced you, that what you are facing is a problem?
- When did the problem begin?
- Where did the problem begin?
- How long has the problem been going on?
- Who or what, do you believe caused the problem?

1st - Step in Problem Solving
Define and identify the problem

There are 2 Types of Problems.

- 1st - Actual Situational Problem
- 2nd - Desired Situational Problem

Actual Situational Problem is another name for Present Situational Problem or Current Situational Problem. This simply means a present situational problem or current situational problem that deals with a problem we are experiencing, and going through at the present moment.

Too many times people allow the problem of their yesterday, and past failures, to interfere into their present moments in life. Actual Situational Problem is an existing problem that you are facing now, and it is taking place in your present moment; the real, true, genuine and authentic moment.

Desired Situational Problem is when someone allows their desire feeling and emotions, that has been impacted by their hurt, pain and bitterness to interfere with an Actual Situational Problem, that really exists (vs.) a Desired Situational Problem, that's not a legitimate problem. This type of person has allowed their emotions to make nothing into something. That was never an Actual Situational Problem in the beginning. So now, this person has allowed their emotions and feelings to escalate nothing into something, that has caused them to be mad, upset, angry, bitter, stressed, frustrated, aggravated and ready to give up all for nothing.

2nd Step in Problem Solving
Determine the Root Cause of the Problem

R.C.A. means Root Cause Analysis. It helps you to analyze the root cause of the problem by using a technique that helps a person to move past (asking questions to answering questions). It helps a person to move pass talking about their problem, to the point of analyzing the problem and determining how to solve the problem using R.C.A. (Root Cause Analysis).

The first thing a problem solver does through R.C.A. is to seek and identify the origin of a problem, using a specific set of steps that helps you find the primary cause of the Problem.

- Step 1 - determine what happened?
- Step 2 - determine why it happened?
- Step 3 - determine what needs to be done and figure out what to do to reduce the likelihood, that the problem will ever happen again.

3rd Step in Problem Solving
Eliminate the Problem

The word eliminate means to completely remove or get rid of something or someone. It also means to do away with, to end, to stop, terminate, destroy, annihilate, and to put out by extinguishing it. The process of elimination is a method of identifying and detecting a process that is a continuation of problems and they must be eliminated because the problem keeps showing up in a person's life, and it's not getting better, but worse.

Luke 8:43-48, talks about a woman with the issue of blood, who had a problem for 12 years, and suffered with that same problem, and better became worse in her life. But she used the Process of Elimination to determine, what she had done for the past 12 years. She determined after paying doctors and spending all of her money that it did not cause her problem to get better, but her problem grew worse.

2 Methods for the Process of Elimination.
In order to eliminate the problem you must first identify the difference between Dissolving Problems (vs.) Resolving Problems.

- Dissolving Problems means to discontinue, it means to bring closure, or an ending to something or someone. Dissolving problems means to no longer invest time, energy or money into something but to simply eliminate the problem. Through the process of elimination you will discover, it is no longer worth the investment. Dissolving problems means the situation is a liability and not worth the investment.

- Resolving a Problem means to settle, or find a solution to the problem or dispute by determining and deciding to renew or bring restoration to the problem. Resolving Problems simply means a person believes that it is worth the investment to give more time, energy, money, and attention to something or someone to resolve a problem. Resolving Problems means the situation is an asset and worth the investment.

EXAMPLES:

- A Car Battery: Sometimes a battery dies because the lights were left on, the door was not completely closed, or the car doesn't start due to bad weather. But you don't have to eliminate a dead battery. The solution is to recharge or jump start the dead battery. By recharging the dead battery, you restore power back into the battery again. This is called (Resolving the Problem).

- <u>Dead Battery:</u> If the dead battery can't be recharged, because it has dead cells in the battery. This means the battery itself has lost life and the ability to keep a charge, therefore the battery must be eliminated rather than continuing to try, and keep recharging it. Eliminating the problem by replacing the old battery with a new battery is called Dissolving the Problem.

4th Step in Problem Solving
Develop and Select Option Solution

When developing and selecting Option Solution for problem solving you must begin by always looking at your problems in a different way. If you continue looking at your problems as you always have, you will only keep getting the same results, and that result will not resolve your problem. Finding new alternatives, options and perspectives, will allow a person to develop and select more options in problem solving.

3 processes for Developing and Selecting the Option Solution.

- 1st – Suitability
- 2nd – Feasibility
- 3rd – Flexibility

Suitability comes from the root word Suitable. (Genesis 2:18 NIV- Suitable Helper) Suitable means acceptable, fitting, and appropriate. It means proven, tried and tested; to pass the test or to guarantee satisfaction.

Suitability Process - Suitability means you are qualified and chosen to resolve the issue as part of your assignment as a problem solver.

1 Samuel 17:33-37, talks about David fighting Goliath. Before he fights Goliath, he gives King Saul his resume which makes him suitable to fight. It explains the why and how he is the right one for the job. David's resume proves that he is suitable and qualified to kill the giant called Goliath, because David has already killed lions and bears. What you have already conquered and overcame in the past, qualifies you to become promoted, suitable and victorious for your future!

1 Samuel 17:38-39, talks about King Saul putting his armor on David to fight Goliath, and how David fell to the ground from the weight of the armor. David said to King Saul, I am not suitable to fight with this armor. As a problem solver you must always know your strengths and weaknesses before engaging into a conflict of solving your problems or someone else's problems.

Feasibility Process - means capable of carrying out the responsibility.

The word feasibility deals with a person being responsible, accountable and credible for the assignment that is given unto them. Feasibility is when your assignment always deals with someone else's problem, and you've been given the responsibility to fix, restore, deliver, minister and bless someone else's brokenness; by being a problem solver (Luke 10:33-35). The Samaritan showed Feasibility.

Flexibility Process - means to be flexible and not easily broken. The process of flexibility requires that have the ability to modify every necessary change, by being transparent, and operating with versatility. Being versatile at every level, as it relates to each and every one's problem on his or her level.

1 Corinthians 9:22-23 GW

22 I became like a person weak in faith to win those who are weak in faith. I have become everything to everyone in order to save at least some of them.

23 I do all this for the sake of the Good News in order to share what it offers.

In understanding flexibility you must be willing to demonstrate that the problems you are facing in your personal life will never interfere with your assignment professionally. To remain a problem solver you cannot be a person that is easily broken.

In dealing with the flexibility process you must first be able to hear the problem, second, understand the problem and third, solve the problem.

5th Step in Problem Solving
Initiate Change

To Initiate Change means to step up and take action without being asked. A person that initiates change always looks for an opportunity to make a difference, because they are not afraid to fail. Initiating Change deals with a person being proactive not reactive. A person that's proactive initiates change according to their assignment and what they believe. A person that's reactive tries to initiate change out of their emotions and how they feel about things or people.

There are 5 Stages to Initiate Change.
1st – Creativity
2nd – Resourceful
3rd – Analytical Thinking
4th – Determination
5th – *Result Oriented* (Strategic Thinker)
Creativity: You must be a creative thinker, planner, organizer, and strategist.

There are 4 processes for Creativity.

- The 1st - is called Idealization

- The 2nd - is called Visualization

- The 3rd - is called Verbalization

- The 4th - is called Materialization/ Manifestation

God did all 4 processes in Creation through creativity.

Idealization is found in Genesis 1:1. In the beginning God had an ideal, a plan, and a purpose. He wanted to create a Heaven and an earth.

Visualization means to visualize or to have a vision. Genesis 1:2, God had a vision, He saw the earth was without form and void and darkness covered the face of the deep, yet God saw light in the midst of the darkness.

Verbalization means to speak, to talk or to say something; God declared and proclaimed in Genesis 1:3, let there be light and in so doing God declared and proclaimed the Laws of the Environment.

Materialization means to come into existence or to materialize, to appear, to become a reality, to take action and watch the invisible become visible and the intangible become tangible.

Genesis 1:21-23, God materialized and manifest a world that started from nothing and made it something. God took nothing and spoke a word until it became the something He spoke.

Stage 1 - Initiate Change - Creativity

- 1st – You must be able to take nothing and make something out of it. Genesis 1:1-3 (Idealization)

- 2nd - You must see the visible, when everyone else see's it invisible. 2 Kings 6:16-17 (Visualization)

- 3rd – You must be able to speak by proclaiming and declaring that all things are possible, when everyone else said it's impossible this is the Law of confession. (Verbalization)

Luke 18:2
2 Jesus said what is impossible with man is possible with God.

- 4th - You must be willing to take a person, that everyone else sees as dirt, and help a person discover their treasures. (Materialization)

Matthew 13:44 NLT
44 The Kingdom of Heaven is like a treasure that a man discovered hidden in a field/dirt. In his excitement, he hid it again and sold everything he owned to get enough money to buy the field.

In order to be a problem solver you have to have creativity, be able to initiate change when everyone else sees a person's life as no good and a low down dirty shame. As a problem solver you have to see the treasure in the person while their life is still in the dirt. - (Materialization)
Stage 2 - Initiate Change - Resourceful to initiate change is to be resourceful. You must be willing to adapt and adopt old problems and turn them into resourceful ideas by being transparent and versatile

always ready to improvise and to find the resources to solve the problem.

John 6:1-14, talks about the feeding of the 5,000, with 2 fish and 5 loaves of bread and how the disciple named Andrew became resourceful.

Stage 3 - Initiate Change - Analytical Thinking - to initiate change you must be an analytical thinker. You must analyze the problem, by being methodical, which means having a systematic structure and order, that holds you accountable. Next, you must be meticulous, which means precise and detailed.

Always pay attention to the details; because the devil is always in the details that's why **Songs of Solomon 2:15 EXB** says,

15 Catch [Grab] the foxes for us—the little foxes that ruin the vineyards while they are in blossom [threats to the relationship].

Luke 13:32 NKJV

32 And He said to them, "Go, tell that fox, 'Behold, I cast out demons and perform cures today and tomorrow, and the third day I shall be perfected.'

The Fox Spirit

The Fox Spirit has a symbolic meaning. Foxes are night creatures, they love creeping in the night, while in the day they have already targeted their prey and who will become their victims. Foxes are sly, clever, sneaky, cunning, deceitful, and crafty. They camouflage themselves to be innocent and harmless, but they are very destructive and dangerous. Both King Solomon and Jesus made mention of the Fox Spirit. Satan is not only a serpent, and a dragon, Satan is also known to be sly as a fox. The foxes can't out run the hound dog, but the fox can outsmart the hound dog; because he knows when the hunter likes to hunt. So he sends the hunter on a false trail. This is what happens many times when we are not analytical thinkers. We allow the fox to outsmart us and to out think us. He causes the little things to destroy the bigger things in our lives which throw us off our destiny and cause us to lose our season of harvest. The devil, like a sly fox; is in the details.

Analytical thinkers always develop a troubleshooting structure for problem solving.

The 1st - Systematic structure of Analytical Thinking is called Diagnostic Evaluation.

The 2nd - Systematic structure of Analytical Thinking is called Prognostic Evaluation.

Diagnostic Evaluation determines the details of what the problem is, by troubleshooting to track down the problem.

Prognostic Evaluation determines not only what the Problem is, but how to solve the problem.

Stage 4 - Initiate Change - Determination

This is where you decide how determined you are in initiating change.

9 Steps to help you determine how to Initiate Change

- **1st – Determination:** You must be determined in what you're doing and where you're going in life.

- **2nd – Inspiration:** You must be inspired by what you're doing and where you're going in life.

- **3rd – Preparation:** You must be prepared about what you're doing and where you're going in life.

- **4th – Dedication:** You must be dedicated about what you're doing and where you're going in life.

- **5th – Sanctification:** You must be set aside for what you're doing and where you're going in life. (You must be willing to sacrifice some things you Love in order to accomplish the things God hates) "God Sacrificed His Son, Whom He Loved."

- **6th – Information:** You must be informed about what you're doing and where you're going in life. (Investigate and research everything that deals with your assignment)

- **7th – Confirmation:** You must be confirmed about what you're doing and where you're going in life. (Make your reservation and keep your confirmation number)

- **8th – Affirmation:** You must be affirmed about what you're doing and where you're going in life by someone that is authorized to give you validation and can consecrate and empower you for the next elevation or promotion.

- 9th – **Destination:** You must have confidence; mentally, physically and spiritually, that all you're doing in life is fulfilling your destiny, that nothing and no one will stop you from accomplishing your destination called destiny.

Romans 8:29-30 NKJV
29 For whom He foreknew, He also predestined to be conformed to the image of His Son, that He might be the firstborn among many brethren.

30 Moreover whom He predestined, these He also called; whom He called, these He also justified; and whom He justified, these He also glorified.

Stage 5 - Initiate Change - Result Oriented Person (Strategic Thinker)
This is a person that has a mindset to get things done. They possess the characteristics of an effective Entrepreneurial Spirit. The Entrepreneurial Spirit is someone who demonstrates true passion for building something great from nothing. They are willing to push themselves to the limits to achieve success. An Entrepreneurial Spirit is a mindset. It's an attitude, an approach to thinking and it actively seeks out change, rather than waiting to adapt to change. It's a mindset that embraces critical questioning, innovation, and continually seeking

improvement, to not only better themselves but the people around them. They take ownership and get things done. They possess energy, growth, and potential. They are team players, they are multi-taskers and they are multi-gifted.

A result oriented person/strategic thinker has the ability to solve problems simply because they are very optimistic, calculating and a risk taker and because they are not afraid of failure.

There are 4 Types of Thinkers.

- The 1st - is a Casual Minded Thinker (A Conservative Person)

- The 2nd - is a Trouble Minded Thinker (Argumentative Person)

- The 3rd - is an Unstable Minded Thinker (Doubting Person)

- The 4th - is a Strategic Minded Thinker (Result Oriented Person)

What type of thinker are you?

The 1st - Type is a "Casual Minded Thinker or a Conservative Person." A casual minded thinker is a conservative person that thinks on an ordinary or average level. This type of thinker is a spiritless thinker, an unexcited thinker, and an immature thinker. This person is too relaxed and unconcerned. So instead of living life at its fullest, they live a part-time life; because this type of person is a temporary, average thinker they accept living a mediocre life.

The 2ⁿᵈ - Type is a "Trouble Minded Thinker" (Argumentative person). This type of thinker always looks for opportunities to cause someone trouble. They are argumentative and they cause unnecessary drama. A Trouble Minded Thinker (Argumentative person) always tries to cause problems and trouble in someone else's life, because they're miserable, lonely, bitter, angry, and full of jealousy. They have nothing good happening in their life and out of envy and strife they will try to sabotage someone else's life by being a trouble maker.

Ezra 4:4-5 NLT
4 Then the local residents tried to discourage and frighten the people of Judah to keep them from their work.(Trouble Makers). 5 They bribed agents to work against them and to frustrate their plans. This went on during the entire reign of King

Cyrus of Persia and lasted until King Darius of Persia took the throne.

A Trouble Minded Thinker/ Argumentative person will always try to cause unnecessary drama, and bring distraction along with division, by sowing (seeds of discord); when God is using you to do something good in your season.

Matthew 13: 25-28 NKJV "Trouble Minded Thinker"- (Argumentative person)
25 but while men slept, his enemy came and Sowed Tares (Seeds of Discord) among the wheat and went his way.

26 But when the grain had sprouted and produced a crop, then the tares also appeared.

27 So the servants of the owner came and said to him, 'Sir, did you not Sow Good Seed in your field? How then does it have tares?'

28 He said to them, 'An enemy has done this.' (Trouble Minded Thinker) The servants said to him, 'Do you want us then to go and gather them up?'

Mark 8:11 ISV
11 The Pharisees arrived and began arguing with Jesus. They tested him by demanding from him a sign from heaven.

Mark 8:11, says the Pharisees argued with Jesus, while Jesus was doing ministry and bring healing and deliverance into so many people's lives, those religious hypocrites argued about the good Jesus was doing, only to bring confusion and distraction, because they deliberately tried to create confusion, by sowing the (seeds of discord).

Stay Focused and Stay Alert!

The 3rd - Type is an "Unstable Minded Thinker" (Doubting Person). The word unstable means unbalanced, deranged, demented, disturbed, and uncertainty. Their life is like sinking sand, which simply means never able to stand or walk in a consistent life style, but take one step forward and they sink in quick sand because of their own distraction.

Genesis 49:3-4 EXB

3 "Reuben, my ·first son [firstborn], you are my strength. Your birth showed I could be a father [ᴸ□…and the first of my virility/vigor]. You have the highest position among my sons [ᴸ□…excelling in pride/rank/authority], and you are the most powerful [ᴸ□…excelling in power].

⁴ But you are ·uncontrolled [unstable] like water [ᶜ□often a symbol of chaos or evil], so you will no longer ·lead your brothers [ᴸ□excel]. This is because you got into your father's bed and ·shamed me by having sexual relations with my slave girl [ᴸ□you defiled it by going up on my couch;.

An unstable minded thinker is a double minded person that lacks confidence. He is a person who has lost their swagger. because this type of thinker is unstable in all their ways.

James 1:8 NLT
8 Their loyalty is divided between God and the world, and they are unstable in everything they do.

An unstable minded thinker is disorderly and full of doubt. A person that is unstable and full of doubt will always second guess themselves and the decisions they make. A person that will always second guess themselves will always second guess and doubt someone else.

John 20:24-29, talks about an unstable and doubting disciple called 'Doubting Thomas'. Thomas doubted Jesus' resurrection even though he was a disciple and follower of Jesus' ministry. Jesus had sent a message to all of His disciples that He had been resurrected, and to meet Him in Galilee, all the other disciples was obedient and showed up where Jesus told them to be; all but doubting Thomas. When the other disciples told doubting Thomas, they had witnessed and saw Jesus' resurrected body, doubting Thomas said, I will not believe that Jesus has been resurrected unless, I see and feel the nailed and scared Hands.

The word Doubt in the Greek terminology means Diakrino, to cancel, to condemn, to terminate and to disqualify yourself. Don't allow your unstable thinking to disqualify you.

The 4th - Type is a Strategic Minded Thinker. (A Result Oriented Person)

A "Strategic Minded Thinker" is like a chess player, who strategizes from the end to the beginning. A strategic minded thinker is like a successful chess player who understands the casualties of war. They understand that sometimes you have to sacrifice your pawns, bishops and knights, just to save your king and queen so that the Kingdom can win and conquer the territory and claim total victory. A strategic minded thinker never lives in the present of the moment, but they always foresee the future moment that's ahead of them, and what it takes to make preparations and win.

A strategic minded thinker is an out of the box thinker. Someone who thinks outside of the norm, average or mediocre. They refuse to be boxed-in and told they can't win, when they know how to articulate, and to be innovative and on the cutting edge. **Mark 2:1-12,** talks about four men that were out of the box thinkers. That took a paralyzed man and picked him up and carried him on the roof top of another man's house, and by thinking outside the box, they tore the roof off another man's house just to get that man to Jesus, so he could be healed. (Their strategic thinking started all because of a crowded house and a backed up line that was going nowhere). (Don't Curse Your Crisis)

It's important to understand what type of thinker you are. A strategic minded thinker will always be a problem solver; all other thinkers will either be a causal minded thinker (conservative person), trouble minded thinker (argumentative person), or an unstable minded thinker (doubting person). If you are not a part of the solution then you are a part of the problem.

For example: If you have a $5,000 problem and you minimize your $5,000 problem on a $500 level, that doesn't solve your problem. Because you have minimized your problem as if it doesn't exist, but the reality is, you are still $4,500 short of solving a $5,000 problem.
Your thinking cannot wish something away, hope something away, cry something away, fuss something away, fight something away, curse something away, or even pray something away, because God gives us the answers to our prayers, and once God gives us the answers, we have to get up and execute, by being obedient and following God's instructions to the letter.

These different types of thinkers will determine if you overcome your financial difficulty, social difficulties, relational difficulties, ministerial difficulty and health difficulties.

6th - Step to Problem Solving
Implementing the Solution for Change

Implementing solution means to educate, empower, and to equip a person on how to move from always fixing their problems to managing and maintaining beyond problems.

Until you learn how to implement the solution for change, you will always go through circles and cycles called process, rather than managing, maintaining and servicing the solution to your problem which allows you to experience progress.

Implement means tools or instruments that equip and empowers you to be successful in your assignment. When you discover what you have been equipped and empowered to do you'll tap into your niche and purpose in life.

The gift and calling that God has ordained you to execute, to utilize and to demonstrate the effectiveness of your assignment in order to implement the solution for change.

To understand, implementing your tools or gifts in order to be successful; you must identify the tools or gifts you are working with.

For example:
A carpenter's implementing tools for building are a hammer, a nail, a skill saw, a ladder, and other hand tools.
A doctor's implementing tools are a stethoscope, a blood pressure monitor, a needle, a thermometer, etc.

A mechanics implementing tools are ratchet sets, wrench sets, socket sets, screw drivers etc.

A football player's implementing tools are a football helmet, a mouth piece, shoulder pads, football cleats, a football, a jersey, and etc.

A Christian or a Believer's implementing tools are a Bible, passion, a prayer life, worship & praise, and the ability to be a soul winner, and more.

What implementing tools are you using to be a problem solver that allows you to implement the solution for change? Do you know what you are gifted to do? Do you know how to implement the tools to do it?

Millionaire Mentality

Chapter 13

Implementing Change

There are 7 stages to implementing solutions for Change while Solving Problems.

1st – Creative Urgency (A Back Up Plan)

2nd – Form a Powerful Coalition (An All-Pro Team)

3rd – Create New Strategy

4th – Communicate the Vision

5th – Remove all Obstacles

6th – Create Short Term Wins

7th – Build on the Change - Outcome Evaluation

The 1st - Stage is called Creative Urgency.
Having a backup plan identifies potential threats and develops solutions to resolve and remove the problem before they occur. Creative Urgency means the quality or condition of being able to make necessary adjustments without panicking, falling apart, and without becoming hysterical under pressure. You must make preparation from (A to Z)

when implementing solutions as a problem solver, and at the same time you must understand no matter how well you prepare and plan, things still goes wrong. Creative Urgency (Backup Plan) deals with having a backup plan or exit strategy. When plan A and B go wrong you must have plan C and D in place to improvise or implement. Creative Urgency is another name for Disaster Recovery Plan. Creative Urgency is creating an exit strategy to escape road blocks, pitfalls, detours and dead ends. Exodus 14:21 says, Moses was given a plan and strategy by God to bring the people out of the bondage of Egypt. He was to lead the people of God through the wilderness, but the Bible says that Moses and the people of God ran into a road block, a dead end; called the Red Sea and Moses had to use Creative Urgency or a Disaster Recovery Plan called Faith in God that caused him not to become hysterical or panic under pressure. Then Moses stretched out his rod and trusted God to give him a Creative Urgency Exit Strategy. God caused the Red Sea to back up on both sides so the people of God could cross over to the other side closer to promise. In spite of how bad things look in your life, you are closer to promise then where you started from!

Do you have an Exit Strategy in place when the unexpected goes wrong? Do you always drive around with your spare tire, just in case you have a flat tire?

The 2nd - Stage - is Forming a Powerful Coalition (An All-Pro Team). An All-Pro Team represents the M.V.P.s (Most Valuable Players) chosen from each team to be placed on another team These individuals are recognized and nominated by their peers or other teammates for the position of M.V.P. (Most Valuable Player) on the team, but also an All-Pro team player. The word Pro means professional and being the best at what they do.

A Coalition represents your team, your allies, and partners who initiate change by taking action that produces one common purpose. The coalition or team must believe no one person is greater than the team. Luke 5:7, they called for their partners to help them. In order to form a powerful coalition or All-Pro Team of Partners Luke 14:28-30 ERV

1st – You must know the environment you are targeting and the time and cost it will take to invest into it.

2nd – You must know the product (Gift) that you are marketing and the expected return on your investment.

3rd – You must know how to implement the tools of your strength and weakness as well as your partners for what it is you are trying to catch or fulfill as it relates to your assignment. In order to understand true partnership or the Power of Coalition, you must be willing in the moment of your partner's weakness or fragilities; to make them look better than they really performed. You must know the play-call, as well as be able to execute the play that has been called without causing a violation or being penalized, which can cause a setback. You must be able to identify who your partners are as it relates to forming a Powerful Coalition. The word coalition means a group of people who join together for a common cause. The word coalition comes from the Latin word (colitio), which means "To Grow Together."

In any partnering of relationships, whether it is companionship, friendship, a partnership for business or partnering for ministry; the partnership or the coalition must be built on planning how "To Grow Together."

There are 5 "A" Factors to consider when forming a Powerful Coalition or Partnership

- The 1st – is called Accountability
- The 2nd – is called Association
- The 3rd – is called Accessibility
- The 4th – is called Assimilation
- The 5th – is called Appreciated Value

These are the 5 qualifications and criteria's of a healthy business partnership and for growing a personal and intimate relationship.

1st – Accountability is the fact or condition of a person being accountable to someone. Never get in a partnership with someone or enter into an intimate relationship with a person that's not willing to show forth accountability, responsibility, dependability and answerability to what they should be accountable for.

2nd – Association means someone you associate with. Never partner in a partnership or enter into an intimate relationship with someone that is not willing to associate with (Anything or Anyone). They will be a liability to the relationship. An association is a group that comes together to organize for a joint purpose.

AMOS 3:3 NLT
Can two people walk together without agreeing on the direction?

Who you associate with reflects your personality, but it determines your integrity. (Birds of a Feather Flock Together)

3rd – Accessibility means Accessible. Never partner with someone or enter into an intimate relationship with someone that has not proven that they are accessible, reliable, consistent, dependable, trustworthy and supporting.

4th – Assimilation means to Assimilate. Never begin a partnership or enter into an intimate relationship with someone that has not proven they can assimilate through assimilation; to be fully understanding; to be able to make adjustments and to be transparent with new ideas, plans, and strategies. Assimilation simply means to be able to make the necessary change.

5th – Appreciated Value means to appreciate something or someone. Never enter into a partnership or an intimate relationship with a person that does not appreciate and understand your worth, time, value, and the sacrifices you make to stay in the relationship. To understand the appreciated value of a partnership means you have predetermined by a person or people; not only their Net-Work but their Net-Worth.

Never be so excited in what you know God has for you in life, and still not be prepared to catch it, and watch it get away. The disciples had caught an abundant supply of fishes; which Jesus had prophesied and proclaimed they would catch; but the reality is what they caught almost got away.

Luke 5:6 says, the net began to break and they called for their "Partners" to help them. It is important to form a powerful coalition (An All-Pro Team) that you can count on. If these men didn't have a powerful team of partners, or the right relationships, with the right people or person that understood the assignment on their life, they would have lost another fulfilled season. The abundance and supply of (fish/blessing) that was proclaimed and declared; by Jesus. The disciples would have lost their fish/blessing that Jesus prophetically prophesied over their life and season. Forming a powerful coalition is good but each of you has to know and understand each other's net-work and new-worth.

When you have the right partners, people, friends, in your life; what God has promised you is yours, and the right people in your life will make sure you don't lose another season that God has promised to you. The right people in your life will help you stay focused, and keep you accountable, so you don't become distracted when it's time for you to "Drag It In" (it being your promise, business, ministry, or your Success for Perpetuity.

The right people in your life, when it's your season will stand by you and will celebrate what you are about to catch. They will say to you, don't lose what you are about to catch in your season but "Drag It In"! This is the season that we're not going to lose another "catch" that God has promised us; because we're assembling ourselves with the right people (All Pro-Players) that are professional, stable, consistent and able to help bring balance in our lives. We declare and proclaim that this is still our season and time for turnaround; for healing, for restoration, and our time of abundance! So, "Drag It In!"

We cannot allow another season to get away, because we have lost patience and become weary in well doing. We must keep the faith along with endurance and hold to the Word of God according to...

Psalms 30:5 AMP
5 For His anger is but for a moment, but His favor is for a lifetime or in His favor is life. Weeping may endure for a night, but joy comes in the morning.

3rd Stage - New Creative Strategy (Expanding the Brand)

In order to implement change you must be an out of the box thinker, and a risk taker. You must be willing at all times to make the necessary adjustments. New Creative Strategy is a method or "plan" chosen to bring about a desired future, such as achievement of a goal or solution to a problem. The name New Creative Strategy is a military term or saying when one is at battle or war and trapped by their enemy, it means to shift formation, change or reposition. It means to begin a new strategic preparation for battle because sometimes our greatest defeat in life, does not know when we have been defeated or what we are doing that is not working, and we're in such denial instead of writing it off as a loss and dismantling it, we continue to throw good money at bad money, and invest more time and energy into a liability.

In business terminology a New Creative Strategy means to cut losses in exchange for capital/money. If you no longer have equity or collateral your investment becomes a liability and high risk, whether it deals with business partnerships, a relationship, a house, a car or whatever it maybe. New creative strategies allow you to do collaborative damage.

Collaborative Damage is damage to things that are incidental to the intended target. Collaborative Damage is a military term where non-combatants are accidently or unintentionally killed or wounded in battle.

Do not confuse Strategic Strategy and New Creative Strategy because New Creative Strategy sometimes means what you had strategized from the beginning through process and time has maximized its potential and capacity to work successfully. It has become outdated and no longer can it be modified under a new modification. So, New Creative Strategies cause a person to expand their brand and label for new modifications as part of contingency planning.

Isaiah 42:9 NKJV
Behold, the former things have come to pass, And New Things I declare; Before they spring forth I tell you of them.

Isaiah 43:19 AMP
Behold, I am doing a New Thing! Now it springs forth; do you not perceive and know it and will you not give heed to it? I will even make a way in the wilderness and rivers in the desert.

If God is doing a new thing that means we are about to receive a new plan of instructions as well as a New Creative Strategy, because God can't do a new thing and we're still performing the old thing.

Isaiah 48:6-7 AMP
6 You have heard [these things foretold], now you see this fulfillment. And will you not bear witness to it? I show you specified New Things from this time forth, even hidden things [kept in reserve] which you have not known. 7 They are Created now [Called into Being by the Prophetic Word], and not long ago; and before today you have never heard of them, lest you should say, Behold, I knew them!

Ephesians 4:22-24 ERV
22 You were taught to leave your old self. This means that you must stop living the evil way you lived before. That old self gets worse and worse, because people are fooled by the evil they want to do. 23 You must be made New in your hearts and in your thinking. 24 Be that New person who was made to be like God, truly good and pleasing to him.

Colossians 3:9-14 MSG
9-11 Don't lie to one another. You're done with that Old life. It's like a filthy set of ill-fitting clothes you've stripped off and put in the fire. Now you're dressed in a New wardrobe. Every item of your New way of life is custom-made by the Creator, with his Label on it. All the Old fashions are now obsolete. Words like Jewish and non-Jewish, religious and irreligious, insider and outsider, uncivilized and uncouth, slave and free, mean nothing. From now on everyone is defined by Christ, everyone is included in Christ.
12-14 So, chosen by God for this New life of love, dress in the wardrobe God picked out for you: compassion, kindness, humility, quiet strength, discipline. Be even-tempered, content with second place, quick to forgive an offense. Forgive as quickly and completely as the Master forgave you. And regardless of what else you put on, Wear Love. It's your basic, all-purpose garment. Never be without it.

Revelation 21:4-5 AMP
4 God will wipe away every tear from their eyes; and death shall be no more, neither shall there be anguish sorrow and mourning nor grief nor pain any more, for the Old conditions and the former

order of things have passed away. **5 And He Who is seated on the throne said, See! I make All Things New. Also He said, Record this, for these sayings are faithful accurate, incorruptible, and trustworthy and true genuine.**

EXPANDING THE BRAND

The word brand means label, stamp, a mark, a type of product manufactured by a particular company under a particular name.

In order to grow the brand or expand the brand you need to know what Grows a successful business, ministry or Partnership.

The 3 "P" Factors to Grow or Expand the Brand.

- 1st – People
- 2nd – Product
- 3rd – Process

The 3 "P" Factors

1st – People: In order to grow and expand the brand, people are the product you target and you must be willing to invest in people. You must be willing to grow the people, in order to grow the business, as well as understand the mindset and culture of the people you target to promote and sponsor the brand.

John 4:4 NKJV
4 But He needed to go through Samaria. Jesus targeted these people as the product and this woman endorsed Jesus brand.

John 4:7 NKJV
7 A woman of Samaria came to draw water. Jesus said to her, "Give Me a drink."

2nd – Product: You must grow the product as well as market the product. You must be willing to improve the product by understanding what the people are in need of as well as what they are searching for.

John 4:10 NKJV
10 Jesus answered and said to her, "If you knew the gift of God, and who it is who says to you, 'Give Me a drink,' you would have asked Him, and He would have given you Living Water."

3rd – Process: You must be willing to respect and understand the process and the people you are servicing. You must also understand the brand, trust the process for developing, manufacturing and becoming distributors for your product.

John 4:28-30 NKJV
28 The woman then left her water pot, went her way into the city, and said to the men, 29 "Come, see a Man who told me all things that I ever did. Could this be the Christ?" 30 Then they went out of the city and came to Him. (The woman Endorsed the Brand to the People of the City).

John 4:39 NKJV
39 And many of the Samaritans of that city believed in Him because of the word of the woman who testified, "He told me all that I ever did."

The people of the city bought into the product because of the "Endorsement" made by the Samaritan woman. You will never expand the brand without discovering what or who your "Endorser" is for the product you are selling. The word endorse means to declare one's public approval or support, to sign a contract of agreement, or to commercialize a product for advertisement. An Endorser is a person who's authorized to sign a negotiable security contract, in order to transfer ownership from one party to another; to approve the terms and conditions of the contract. The word endorsement means the act of giving one's public approval or support to someone or something. It means to back something or someone; to have their approval, recommendation, sanctioning, affirmation, buy in, and exclusive support.

You will never be successful building or expanding a brand without endorsements, endorsers or someone to endorse the Product. When you understand the brand of Nike tennis shoes it's the most successful tennis shoe company in the world because it was built on the success of not only the brand but finding successful athletes, celebrities and stars to endorse and promote their product. So, when you think of Nike tennis shoes and their brand as well as slogan and Label; who do you think of first? Do you think of all the athletes and stars such as Michael Jordan, LeBron James, Kobe Bryant, Tiger Woods, Serena Williams and others that have endorsed Nike's product and brand or do you think of the owner, (Phil Knight) who's Net-Worth is 23.9 billion dollars. The reason (Phil Knight) is so wealthy and a multi-billionaire, is because he built his brand on people that would endorse his product as well as commercialize and broadcast his product. Phil had a

New Creative Strategy on how to sale his Brand through different endorsers.

When you think about Facebook, its brand and its endorsers what is the first thing that comes to your mind? Is it all your social media friends, or Facebook status followers?; when you think about the Brand called Facebook, do you think about the owner, (Mark Zuckerberg) and he expanded his brand and how it is now worth 28.4 billion dollars because he understood the 3 "P" Factors; people, product and process. Facebook is designed to target people that sale their product through social media. It is designed for you to gather associates and friends and to build followers through your relationships, likes and dislikes. Mark Zuckerburg trusted the process of expanding the brand using you as an endorser

When you think of Microsoft, what is the first thing that comes to mind? Is it a computer desktop, laptop computer or software, or do you think about the founder, (Bill Gates) who has accumulated a net-worth of 81 billion dollars all because he expanded his brand successfully using the 3 "P" Factors. He targeted people, he marketed his product by expanding to a greater level of technology and he helped to revolutionize the 21st century concept of how the world would shift in doing business from pencil, paper and typewriters. He was able to advance his new concepts through new creative strategies for doing business; simply because he trusted the people, the product, and the process when no one else believed in the process.

Bill Gates tried to sell his idea to a giant company called IBM at the time but they laughed at him and rejected his product and process. Now, IBM is no longer the giant thriving company of the world called technology, because they could not see Bill Gates' New Creative Strategy. In 1985 Bill Gates launched Microsoft Windows Software application and it changed the world of technology and now much of the world does business using Microsoft Windows. Today, Bill Gates is worth over 81 billion dollars, and each year he gives 1 billion dollars back into charity and into ministries and businesses that are on the cutting edge to bring forth New Creative Strategies.

When we look back at the beginning of time and creation, endorsement and expanding the brand or labeling did not start with Phil Knight, owner of Nike, Mark Zuckerberg, owner of Facebook, or Bill Gates, owner of Microsoft Software, it began with God Himself.

According to Genesis in the beginning God looked over a world without form, shape and definition and God became the Endorser and He endorse a world through New Creative Strategy and God began to create a new world and a new order with His New Creative Strategy. When He finished His new creative strategy and planning for expanding his brand, He began to search for someone to "Endorse," His product and to endorse His brand; someone that would become a spokesman to help communicate and sell His product. Someone that could explain the brand by communicating how the plan and product works. Then God created a man and a woman, to become the new endorsers that would represent God's expanding brand called earth. Later, the Bible says in the book of Genesis that God is about to destroy the old brand called earth and He searched for someone he could establish a new endorsement agreement with, someone that could endorse the brand..

Genesis 6:8 NKJV
8 But Noah found grace in the eyes of the Lord.

Every time God is about to expand His brand He always searches to find a new endorser. The next time we find God beginning to expand his brand is in Genesis chapter 12. He looks for a new endorser He calls out to one by the name of Abraham, to leave his country, family, his old customs and ways of doing things, and to step out on faith to expand the brand. As we search through the Word of God we always see God doing business, expanding his brand and labeling, but he always searched or called on someone to endorse the brand. In Matthew 3:17, we find God again expanding his brand and finding a new endorser. The Bible says in Matthew 3:17, Jesus shows up at the Jordan with John the Baptist to be baptized and once He comes up out of the water, and the Heavens open up, the C.E.O. endorses His new endorser, His son, Jesus who would become the face of His expanded brand. God spoke and said this is My Beloved Son whom I 'Endorse' as the face and label of my expanding brand and in whom I am well pleased.

In Matthew 17:5, we see the C.E.O. is expanding the brand again on Mt. Transfiguration. Jesus takes His three intercessors Peter, James and John up with Him to show them the new product by taking off His human flesh called humanity and exposing His divinity to His three intercessors; called Glory; which is the new and improved product. Once Peter, James and John awake from sleeping, Peter asked Jesus could he build three Tabernacles: One for Jesus, One for Moses, One for Elijah and then the C.E.O.(God) speaks and interrupts Peter's program, and reminds them that Jesus is the face of the brand and He's the one that He is endorsing. God says, 'this is My Beloved Son whom I "Endorsed" hear ye Him!' Matthew 4:19, we see Jesus expanding the brand by choosing and selecting 12 men to endorse the new product called the 12 Disciples/Apostles.

We must understand, if we are going to build something successful and be more successful, we must be willing and able to expand the brand, but we will only be successful when we partner and connect with people that know how to endorse our product and represent the quality of our brand!

4th Stage – Communicate the Vision
What is your why?

The fourth stage of implementing solutions for change while solving problems is called "Communicate the Vision". At this level you have to be able to explain your vision through a variety of communication outlets as well as what determines your success.

Habakkuk 1:1 NKJV
1 The burden which the prophet Habakkuk saw.

1st - You must discover your burden and passion for your ministry. (Why Factor)

Habakkuk 1:2-4 ERV
2 Lord, I continue to ask for help. When will you listen to me? I cried to you about the violence, but you did nothing! 3 People are stealing things and hurting others. They are arguing and fighting. Why do you make me look at these terrible things? 4 The law is weak and not fair to people. Evil people win their fights against good people. So the law is no longer fair, and justice does not win anymore.

2nd - You must be able to carry the (Burden) and (Responsibility) of your ministry, without complaints or complaining.

Habakkuk 2:2-3 EXB
2 The Lord answered me: "Write down the Vision; write it ·clearly [plainly] on clay tablets so whoever reads it can run to tell others. 3 It is not yet time for the message to come true [For the Vision awaits an appointed time], but that time is coming soon [it hastens to the end; or it speaks about the end]; the message will ·come true [not lie]. It may seem like a long time, but [Though it

tarries/lingers] be patient and wait for it, because it will surely come; it will not be delayed.

3rd - You must be able to communicate and explain the vision, your ability to explain your vision will determine how successful you will be when you complete your assignment.

Habakkuk felt the burden, the pain, hurt, and suffering of the people he was assigned to help and minister too. When you experience carrying the burden and passion for people that you know, and don't know; it causes you to wake up with the burden, go throughout the day with that burden on you, and fall asleep with the same burden. This burden is called passion and compassion that has awakened your gift for ministry.

In the first chapter of Habakkuk, he discovered his burden and passion when he saw and heard about hurting and broken people that were trying to do the best that they could in life, and was still failing to prosper. Habakkuk also saw an evil and bad set of people that was living and doing anything in life, and it appeared that they were succeeding and prospering. Habakkuk cried out unto the Lord and he began to intercede with a burden and passion for the people. He asked God 'where is the justice, why aren't you doing something about this?'

Habakkuk chapter 2:2-3, Habakkuk was corrected, rebuked, and instructed by God what to do, by revealing to Habakkuk His instructions. God told Habakkuk in order to get passed the burden and the passion of hurting, broken, and suffering people, you must be able to communicate the vision, as well as explain the vision, through explanation that will determine their success to turn their life around.

The word vision in Greek terminology is (vi`dere). It means supernatural sights; it also means a sense of sight or foresight. This means seeing without seeing. In Mark 10:46-48, blind Bartimaeus saw without seeing because he operated in a supernatural vision. Despite being on the road in Jericho, a place of spiritual warfare. Bartimaeus was still able to give God the praise without seeing his deliverance, without seeing his healing, without seeing his blessing. Because of (vi`dere) having supernatural sight or a sense of sight and Barak which means to sense triumph, sense victory without physically seeing it he supernaturally saw it in the spirit realm and was able to communicate the vision and explain the vision through "praise." This determined Blind

Bartimaeus' success that released his complete deliverance.

5th Stage – Remove All Obstacles

The 5th stage is called Remove all Obstacles. You must be willing and courageous enough to remove all hindrances, barriers, stumbling blocks, and anything that will keep you from reaching your perpetuity for success.

God told Moses and Joshua to remove all obstacles in Canaan that kept them out of the Promise Land for 40 years. Obstacles are things or people that block one's way or impedes and hinders progress; such as barriers, hurdles, stumbling blocks, obstructions, impediments, hindrances, snags, drawbacks, hitch or hick-ups. It means to be handicapped by dysfunction, complications, difficulties, problems, disadvantages, and dead ends.

The road map to success is learning how to navigate around every obstacle you face, or every obstacle that confronts you, by making necessary the adjustments. There are two major obstacles that you must be willing to overcome to receive success and they are fear and self-doubt. The 1st major obstacle is called the fear of failure. The Fear of Failure has caused many gifted and talented people to fail and to live a life of embarrassment and rejection. It causes one to believe that they will forever live in poverty and that they will always be a loser instead of a winner. This is why so many people give up so easily, because as soon as they try to reach their goals in life, while trying to have something and be someone in life, the Fear of Failure overwhelms them like a bucket of water on a small fire, and extinguishes their dreams completely.

The 2nd major obstacle is called self-doubt. Self-doubt is a mental collapse in one's thinking that paralyzes all their decisions. It not only causes one to live in fear but in doubt about who they are. It causes one to disqualify themselves from even trying to achieve and receive what God has promised them in life.

Matthew 14:30, Self–Doubt became Peter's obstacle as well as his hurdle. It caused him to become distracted and to lose focus of the success he was having while walking on the water and doing the impossible. Fear and self-doubt will always be the two major obstacles that we must overcome, if we are ever going to fulfill our dreams and destiny in life.

5 Types of Obstacles/Factors to Avoid Pitfalls.

- The 1st – is called Corrective Action Planning and Preventive Action Planning.

- The 2nd – is called The Lack of Cooperation.

- The 3rd – is called The Lack of Measurement/Giving.

- The 4th – is called The Lack of Reporting.

- The 5th – is called Let's Build a Bridge and Get Over It!

Corrective Action Planning means action to Identify and eliminate any reoccurrence or repeated problems. Preventive Action Planning means removing any perceivable threats, danger or obstacles, that will delay and cause any distractions concerning your assignment. It means to re-think or re-structure the process for a better result.

Corrective Action Planning is discovering where one went wrong and how to correct the wrong and make it right (vs.) Preventive Action Planning, looks ahead at future potential threats, and becomes the forerunner that makes sure that anything or anyone that could cause futuristic harm or danger will be eliminated. Before it has a chance to manifest, and present itself as a problem.

Ezekiel 37, God speaks to the Prophet Ezekiel about re-thinking or re-structuring the process of Corrective Action Planning and Preventive Action Planning.

The 1st – thing God asked Ezekiel was can these bones live that are dead? Ezekiel's response to God was "you know". God gave Ezekiel instructions on how to bring forth Corrective Action Planning and Preventive Action Planning through the use of the re-structuring process. God instructed the Prophet Ezekiel, to take a broken structure, that had been dried up, separated, and divided with broken people, who had lost their spirit and power, and to implement a new corrective action plan that would bring forth a new process, to educate, empower, equip, and breathe new life, and a new spirit, and new preventive action planning!

2nd – A Lack of Cooperation is an obstacle that you must be willing to remove as well as obstacles called lack, slack, and laziness that cause people to become complainers, whiners and insensitive about what must be done and the part they must contribute to see it get done. The lack of cooperation is an obstacle and a stumbling block that caused the children of Israel to wander in the wilderness for 40 years because of their lack of cooperation.

The people that followed Moses, praised God and celebrated God as long as God was providing miracles and blessings, but when it was time to trust God, serve God, and to follow God with obedience by following the man servant called Moses; who God placed over their life; the people of God became lack, slack and lazy. They caused stagnation and delay, not only to the Will of God but the Promises of God.

2 Peter 3:9 NKJV
9 The Lord is not slack concerning His Promise, as some count slackness, but is longsuffering toward us, not willing that any should perish but that all should come to repentance.

2 Peter 3:9 AMP
9 The Lord does not delay and is not tardy or slow about what He Promises, according to some people's conception of slowness, but He is long-suffering (extraordinarily patient) toward you, not desiring that any should perish, but that all should turn to repentance.

The people of God missed the fulfillment of the promise land for 40 years. When they should have reached the promised land that God had promised them in less than four days to four months. They should have reached the promised land in four days, and they should have conquered and possessed the land in four months. What should have taken four days to four months to fulfill their assignment, ended up taking 40 years to accomplish, because of the obstacle called the Lack of Cooperation.

3rd – A Lack of Measurement/Giving: In order to deal with removing the obstacle called a Lack of Measurement/Giving, you must be willing to measure the results of strategic evaluation and implementation; because numbers never lie! You must be able to measure the results of the time, sacrifice, investment and cost; you have put into the work or the assignment to reap a harvest.

The Key to Measuring Success, is Giving to Get Results!
In order to remove obstacles you have to be willing to give to get results that will manifest good measure and increase your capacity. You must be willing to give more time, sacrifice, dedication, commitment, forgiveness, love, and yes even money, in order to get a return on your investment.

Luke 6:38 NKJV
38 Give, and it will be given to you: good measure, pressed down, shaken together, and running over will be put into your bosom. For with the same measure that you use, it will be measured back to you."

Luke 6:38 EXB
38 Give, and you will receive [it will be given to you]. You will be given much [a good measure]. Pressed down [Compacted], shaken together, and running over, it will spill into your lap [the image is of grain overflowing its container]. The way you Give to [standard/measure you use with] others is the way God will Give to [standard/Measure God will use with] you.

1 Kings 17:13-14 TLB
13 But Elijah said to her, "Don't be afraid! Go ahead and cook that 'last meal,' but bake me a little loaf of bread first; and afterwards there will still be enough food for you and your son.

14 For the Lord God of Israel says that there will always be Plenty of Flour and Oil Left in Your

Containers until the time when the Lord sends rain and the crops grow again!"

Romans 12:3 NLT
Because of the privilege and authority God has given me, I Give each of you this warning: Don't think you are better than you really are. Be honest in your Evaluation of yourselves, measuring yourselves by the faith God has given us.

Ephesians 4:7 GW
7 God's favor has been given to each of us. It was measured out to us by Christ who gave it.

The 4th – is called The Lack of a Reporting Structure.

In order to remove the obstacle called the lack of reporting, you must establish a reporting structure that creates accountability, responsibility and credibility. You will never reach your goals in life, your dreams in life or complete an assignment in life, without a reporting structure.   A reporting structure reveals and exposes what one is doing, what is not being done and what one is doing that is successful.

We discover the reporting system and instructions given by God to Moses; Moses gave to the leaders of the tribes of Israel that were sent out as 12 Spies to investigate the Promise Land, and come back with a report according to;

Numbers 13:30-32 ERV
30 Caleb told the people near Moses to be quiet. Then Caleb said, "We should go up and take that land for ourselves. We can easily take that land."

31 But the men who had gone with him said, "We cannot fight those people! They are much stronger than we are."

32 So those men gave a Report that discouraged the people. They said, "The land we saw is full of strong people. They are strong enough to easily defeat anyone who goes there.

When the 12 spies came back they were suppose to give a Prognostic Praise Report of the Promise Land, flowing with complete success and prospering in total wealth; but out of the 12, only 2 of the spies came back with a good report. The other 10 spies came back with a bad report and discouraged the whole congregation of Israel. This bad report caused the people of God to miss the promise for 40 years.

Joshua 2:1 MSG
1 Joshua son of Nun secretly sent out from Shittim two men as Spies: "Go. Look over the land. Check out Jericho." They left and arrived at the house of a harlot named Rahab and stayed there.

Joshua 2:23 TLB
23 Then the two spies came down from the Mountains and Crossed the river (Bridging the Gap) and Reported to Joshua all that had happened to them.

40 years later, Joshua sent out two spies to investigate and seek out promise. The two spies came back with a prognostic praise report saying not only is the Promise Land everything God has promised us, but we are ready to take it now.

The Difference between Moses Leadership Ministry (vs.) Joshua Leadership of Ministry.

<u>Moses - Type of Leadership Ministry</u>

Moses sent out leaders/spies that went into the Promise Land and brought back a bad report of why, they couldn't complete their assignment. Because Moses' leaders, talked more about the problems of why, they couldn't have what God Promised them. This caused them to go into a 40 year cycle of failures.

Joshua - Type of Leadership Ministry

Joshua sent out leaders/spies that went out into the Promise Land and brought back a good report of how to complete their assignment and possess the Promise Land. Joshua's leaders talked more about the promise of success rather than the problems that continue to lead to failures.

7 Stages to Implement Solution for Change while Solving Problems

6th Stage – Create Short-Term Wins

Nothing motivates a person more than success. Give yourself a taste of victory early while you are implementing your change process. It will make you much hungrier for the next taste of victory.

Psalms 34:8 AMP
8 O Taste and see that the Lord [our God] is good! Blessed (happy, fortunate, to be envied) is the man who trusts and takes refuge in Him.

Very little encourages and gives people confidence more than success gives your ministry, business, or relationships. Short-Term wins should come between one month and one year, depending on the type of changes you implement. Short-term wins, are designed to target early victories, and help you reach your long term goals. Short-term wins help you to turn failures into successes by reaching targets that are achievable with little room for failure. More early victories will produce more confidence, motivation, and inspiration; causing your long term goals to become more believable.
(Change is a habit, cultivate it!)

How to Implement Short-Term Wins.
1st – You Must Prepare
Develop Objectives - You must be open-minded. You can't be influenced by personal feelings and you can't be opinionated. Identify your resources; money, help and net-working partners. Identify and assess the accountability of each person that is a part of the team.

2nd – Focus
- Identify Issues and Opportunities
- Identify Preventive Action Planning Solutions
- Identify and estimate Cost

3rd – You Start
Identify short-term win goals and then give the short-term win goals a deadline for completion.

4th – Deploy
- Agree what your role will be and stay responsible.
- Agree on how you plan on accomplishing your goals and deliver on the promissory.
- Prepare Action Plans and Deadlines

You can have a moment of success and begin to recycle success for so many times, until even success will turn into failure, if you don't learn the new formula on how to improve success on a new level.

5th – Measure Improvement
- Improve Quality
- Improve Cost
- Improve Process Time which is the total time from the beginning to the end of your process.
- Improve Customer Service - serve with the Spirit

of excellence and integrity.
- Recognize Results and Team Efforts (Grade Yourself)

Genesis 26 talks, about a man named Isaac, who needed to create a short-term win, for an early taste of victory. Isaac was in a double famine, and he was on the verge of giving up and losing everything. Isaac was in the process of going back to Egypt a place called Bondage, God told Isaac do not go back to Egypt to the place of bondage and debt; because what you're experiencing is a temporary problem and God has the answer for your permanent solution.

Genesis 26:1-3 AMP
1 And there was a famine in the land, other than the former famine that was in the days of Abraham. And Isaac went to Gerar, to Abimelech king of the Philistines.

2 And the Lord appeared to him and said, Do not go down to Egypt; live in the land of which I will tell you.

3 Dwell temporarily in this land, and I will be with you and will Favor You With Blessings; for to

you and to your descendants I will give all these lands, and I will perform the oath which I swore to Abraham your father.

Genesis 26:12-13 AMP

12 Then Isaac Sowed Seed in that land and received in the same year a hundred times as much as he had planted, and the Lord Favored Him With Blessings.

13 And the man became great and gained more and more until he became very wealthy and Distinguished;

Isaac for years lived among the Philistine's who were his neighbors; without any conflicts or problems, but as soon as Isaac decided to have more, do more, invest more, and grow more, he discovered, these same neighbors called Philistines would soon become his greatest enemies.

Many times in life we find out the people that we associate with, or affiliate with, have no problem with us, until we decide to make more out of our life, or have more in life.

Isaac discovered that his neighbors were his enemies, his friend were his enemies, and his associates were his enemies. You will never know your true enemy until you expose or reveal your true self. Isaac created for himself short-term wins by understanding three processes for early victories. Isaac's 1st - process for short-term wins was called "Earned Income Process for Sowing."

Through this "Earned Income Process for Sowing" Isaac took a (common seed) and in return, received an (uncommon harvest.) This "Earned Income Seed for Sowing" caused Isaac to produce his harvest.

Seed x Time = Harvest (100 Times the Return)

Isaac received a 100 times return on his investment, in the same year.

Genesis 8:22 ERV
22 As long as the earth continues, there will always be a time for planting and a time for harvest. There will always be cold and hot, summer and winter, day and night on earth."

The 2nd – process is investing in your inheritance. (Future) Isaac invested his inheritance.

Genesis 26:18 AMP

18 And Isaac dug again the Wells of Water which had been dug in the days of Abraham his father, for the Philistines had stopped them after the death of Abraham; and he gave them the names by which his father had called them.

Isaac begins to re-dig the wells that his father Abraham had left him for an inheritance. Isaac invested his future into wells that were full of dirt. He discovered how to focus on the water not the dirt. Too many times we become distracted, and lose focus on our investment, because we focus more on the dirt and not the water. Focusing on the dirt represents the dirt that people are throwing on you, that's called negativity and criticism. The dirt is trying to assassinate your character, gift, calling, assignment, dreams, and future leading you to focus more on the dirt and not the water. The water represents the Spirit and life of a person that is trying to tap into their resources and dig up the truth. This truth will help them to capitalize on their investment and release an incredible flow of abundance. So, focus on the water, not the dirt that the enemy is throwing at you.

The 3rd – Process is growing your earnings and investing into four Sources of Income.

Genesis 26:13 AMP
13 And the man became Great and Gained More and More until he became Very Wealthy and Distinguished;

Isaac became successful, prosperous, rich and very wealthy. This is simply because Isaac learned how to grow his earned income and his investment into four sources of income. His investment caused his money to not only multiply, but to accumulate, increase, and make more room for him.

Genesis 26:16-22 AMP
16 And Abimelech said to Isaac, Go away from us, for you are much mightier than we are.

17 So Isaac went away from there and pitched his tent in the Valley of Gerar, and   dwelt there.

18 And Isaac dug again the wells of water which had been dug in the days of   Abraham his father, for the Philistines had stopped them after the death of   Abraham; and he gave them the names by which his father had called them.

19 Now Isaac's servants dug in the valley and found there a well of living [spring] water.

20 And the herdsmen of Gerar quarreled with Isaac's herdsmen, saying, The water is ours. And he named the well Esek [contention] because they quarreled with him.

21 Then [his servants] dug another well, and they quarreled over that also; so he named it Sitnah [enmity].

22 And he moved away from there and dug another well, and for that one they did   not quarrel. He named it Rehoboth [room], saying, For now the Lord has made room for us, and we shall be fruitful in the land.

7th Stage in Problem Solving
Evaluate the Outcome / Build on the Change
It's Not Where You've Been; it's Where You're Going!

Outcome Evaluation
Outcome Evaluation is not when you stare the present moment of today in the face, and hope you get through it without losing your mind, or having a nervous breakdown, but outcome evaluation is when you stare the future in the face, see and declare the end from the beginning because; you understand and

know how and when and where to start and what it takes to finish.

Isaiah 46:10 VOICE
10 From the beginning I declare how things will end; from times long past, I tell what is yet to be, saying: "My intentions will come to pass. I will make things happen as I determine they should."

Psalms 23:5 NCV
5 You prepare a meal for me in front of my enemies. You pour oil of blessing on my head; you fill my cup to overflowing.

Hebrews 12:2 TLB
2 Keep your eyes on Jesus, our leader and instructor. He was willing to die a shameful death on the cross because of the joy he knew would be his afterwards; and now he sits in the place of honor by the throne of God.

Outcome Evaluation is a systematic evaluation of the outcomes set in the stated goals, with a systematic evaluation process using the tools to implement goals, plans, and assignments, with deadlines.

The Evaluation Process for Outcome Evaluation

- The 1st – Evaluation: Where Is the Problem?
- The 2nd– Evaluation: What Caused the Problem?
- The 3rd– Evaluation: Can you Fix the Problem/ How much will it cost you to Fix it?
- The 4th– Evaluation: Can you Afford the Problem/ or is the Problem Worth Fixing?
- The 5th – Evaluation: Outcome Evaluation Solution and Solving Problems

If the problem isn't worth the time and investment dissolve and resolve the problem by dismissing it or letting it go. If the problem is worth your time and investment, continue to invest time and resources, until your problem manifest into your Promise.

4 Steps to Outcome/Impact Evaluation

- INPUT
- OUTPUT
- OUTCOME
- IMPACT

Input means the Act of Processing time and resources. Output means the Act of Progressing time and resources. Outcome means the end results and the conclusion of what was discovered before you ever began. Impact means creating impact factors for investment, and protecting your present and future investment, by always creating residual income, by re- investing into perpetuity for more success!

Genesis 41:30-40 TLB
30 But afterwards there will be seven years of famine so great that all the prosperity will be forgotten and wiped out; famine will consume the land.

31 The famine will be so terrible that even the memory of the good years will be erased.

32 The double dream gives double impact, showing that what I have told you is certainly going to happen, for God has decreed it, and it is going to happen soon.

33 My suggestion is that you find the wisest man in Egypt and put him in charge of administering a nationwide farm program.

34-35 Let Pharaoh divide Egypt into five administrative districts, and let the officials of these districts gather (20%) into the royal storehouses all the excess crops of the next seven years,

36 so that there will be enough to eat when the seven years of famine come. Otherwise, disaster will surely strike."

37 Joseph's suggestions were well received by Pharaoh and his assistants.
38 As they discussed who should be appointed for the job, Pharaoh said, "Who could do it better than Joseph? For he is a man who is obviously filled with the Spirit of God."

39 Turning to Joseph, Pharaoh said to him, "Since God has revealed the meaning of the dreams to you, you are the wisest man in the country!

40 I am hereby appointing you to be in charge of this entire project. What you say goes, throughout all the land of Egypt. I alone will outrank you."

Joseph was chosen by his father Jacob to wear the coat or robe of many colors; which represented multi-gift, multi-purposed and multi-favored. Which meant Joseph had to be able to multi-task in his assignment, but during his assignment Joseph went through an evaluation process by God, to come into a season of maturity in his life where he could evaluate the outcome.

The Joseph Model: 4 Stages of Evaluation Succession Planning

The 1st – is called Input Evaluation. Where Joseph processed time and resources.

The 2nd - is called Output Evaluation. Where Joseph progressed time and resource.

The 3rd - is called Outcome Evaluation. Where Joseph created a deadline for the return on investment after the 1st- 7yrs. (vs.) the next 7yrs.

The 4th– is called Impact Results. This is where Joseph created impact factors for the investment that brought forth unlimited residual and perpetuity of success.

Joseph had the gift of administration, where he administered the gift of governing financial and spiritual interpretation, He was gifted to define the future economy and to interpret dreams and visions. The favor of God rested so heavy on Joseph's life that he found favor with all of his enemies. Joseph was released from death row prison by Pharaoh so he could interpret the dreams God gave Pharaoh that caused the world to change.

Pharaoh promoted Joseph to the office of C.F.O. (Chief Financial Officer). Joseph came up with a 7 year Short-Term Plan, to start a food ministry collecting 20% of all the food that was taken up in the 1st – 7 years. After 7 years Joseph's Long-Term Plan was to take the food ministry and turn it into a supermarket or a (Super Wal-mart). He transformed his food ministry into a fortune 500 Enterprise by saving 20% for 7 years. In other words, Joseph budgeted the food supply by saving 20% of earned income for the 1st – 7 years. Then Joseph took the next 7 years of the 20% savings and earned a 100% return all because he did an investment evaluation or projection.

The 1st - 7 years Joseph taught the people how to take 20% of their earned income, budget and save it for 7 years; but the next 7 years Joseph taught the people how to do Outcome Evaluation. He told them to take the 20% that they had saved and to invest it for the next 7 (bad) years. Take what you have saved and re-invest it.

Joseph revealed and interpreted Pharaoh's dream, he told him how to budget and invest the 20% using Outcome Evaluation through a 14 year process.

1st - Joseph told Pharaoh in the 7 good years of harvest, take 20% of your earned income, budget and save it.

2nd – Joseph told Pharaoh for the next 7 bad harvest years take the 20% that you saved and invest it in the bad season.

Budget Income Investment
Hebrews 5:11-14 MSG
11-14 I have a lot more to say about this, but it is hard to get it across to you since you've picked up this bad habit of not listening. By this time you ought to be teachers yourselves, yet here I find you need someone to sit down with you and go over the basics on God again, starting from square one—baby's milk, when you should have been on solid food long ago! Milk is for beginners, inexperienced in God's ways; solid food is for the mature, who have some practice in telling right from wrong.

A Seven Year Savings Outcome
Matthew 13:3-9 ERV

3 Then Jesus used stories to teach them many things. He told them this story:
"A farmer went out to sow seed.

4 While he was scattering the seed, some of it fell by the road. The birds came and ate all that seed.

5 Other seed fell on rocky ground, where there was not enough dirt. It grew very fast there, because the soil was not deep.

6 But when the sun rose, it burned the plants. The plants died because they did not have deep roots.

7 Some other seed fell among thorny weeds. The weeds grew and stopped the good plants from growing.

8 But some of the seed fell on good ground. There it grew and made grain. Some plants made 100 times more grain, some 60 times more, and some 30 times more.

9 You people who hear me, listen!"

7 Yr. Savings Outcome (vs.) 7 Yr. Investment
Outcome

Genesis 47:15-17 TLB
**15 When the people were out of money, they
came to Joseph crying again for food. "Our
money is gone," they said, "but give us bread; for
why should we die?"**

**16 "Well then," Joseph replied, "give me your
livestock. I will trade you food in exchange."**

**17 So they brought their cattle to Joseph in
exchange for food. Soon all the horses, flocks,
herds, and donkeys of Egypt were in Pharaoh's
possession.**

Genesis 47:18-22 TLB
**18 The next year they came again and said, "Our
money is gone, and our cattle are yours, and
there is nothing left but our bodies and land.**

**19 Why should we die? Buy us and our land and
we will be serfs (Slave Labors) to Pharaoh. We
will trade ourselves for food, then we will live,
and the land won't be abandoned."**

**20 So Joseph bought all the land of Egypt for
Pharaoh; all the Egyptians sold him their fields**

because the famine was so severe. And the land became Pharaoh's.

21 Thus all the people of Egypt became Pharaoh's serfs (Slave Labors.)

22 The only land he didn't buy was that belonging to the priests, for they were assigned food from Pharaoh and didn't need to sell.

Genesis 47:23-30 TLB

23 Then Joseph said to the people, "See, I have bought you and your land for Pharaoh. Here is grain. Go and sow the land.

24 And when you harvest it, a fifth (20%) of everything you get belongs to Pharaoh. (Perpetuity) Keep four parts for yourselves (20%) to be used for next year's seed, and as food for yourselves and for your households and little ones."

25 "You have saved our lives," they said. "We will gladly be the serfs (Slave Labors) of Pharaoh."

26 So Joseph made it a law throughout the land of Egypt—and it is still the law—that Pharaoh

should have as his tax 20 percent of all the crops except those produced on the land owned by the temples.

Outcome Evaluation

Joseph told Pharaoh to teach the people that were under him to save 20% of their money for 7 years. But the people that submitted under Joseph and Pharaoh were disobedient; that after the 7 good years of harvest, entering into the 7 bad years, they had nothing to show for it.

In developing your plan there are 4 things you have to understand about money.

- Income Plan
- Spending Plan
- Savings Plan
- Investment Plan

Income Plan

What is your source of income? How can you increase your current source of income? What additional source of income is possible?

Savings Plan

Where will the savings plan come from each week and year? How much are you planning on saving, weekly, monthly and yearly? Set your goals based upon how much you're planning on bringing in.

Investment Plan

Determine your strategy for creating a residual. Residual is the value of a fixed asset that measures a continuation of return on ever increasing money. This means you're not living off income or salary, you always have money coming in, an ever flowing increase.

Investing is what Isaac did in **Genesis 26:1-12.** He invested in that land and in that same year he received 100 times more in residual by creating an investment plan.

1st - In his process he was successful.

2nd - He was prosperous.

3rd - He was wealthy.

It all started in a time of bad recession that created a double famine in the land. Isaac took his seed (investment) and created a harvest. Tap into your investment wealth.

Thank You:

Although there is much more to add, we pray that you are blessed by the words of this book and by the Spirit of God that has given utterance, clarity and the anointing to say the things that were said and to teach the things that were taught. God's word has so much to offer concerning strongholds and the keys to having the mind of a conqueror. We pray that this book will cause you to study and to learn more about what He (God) has to say.

We also would like to thank you for choosing this book to read. We know that you had many choices when you found this book but we know that it was God's divine Spirit that led you to choose this book on strongholds, so we thank you.

You can learn more about Apostle Tommy R. Twitty online at www.trtministries.com, on facebook at Tommy R. Twitty or at his local church website www.wodca.org. To book Apostle Twitty as a speaker or for your next event, program, or conference please contact us at tommytwitty@yahoo.com or call 864-461-7178.

About the Author:

Apostle Tommy R Twitty

"An anointed vessel of God,

seeking the heart of God for God's people"

A visionary, teacher, prophet, author and founder of TRT Ministries and Reaching Outside the Walls Ministry (R.O.T.W.). He is a native of Chesnee, South Carolina, the Apostle of Word of Deliverance Assemblies in Gaffney, S.C. and Word Church Atlanta in Forest Park, GA. Apostle Twitty is a devoted husband and father to his lovely wife, Elect Lady Nicole Humphries Twitty, their three beautiful children, Shante', Rashawn, Amber and grandson, Braylon.

The Word of Deliverance Assemblies is a youthful, multi-cultural, soul-winning ministry with a message of love, healing and deliverance where "All People of All Races are Freely Welcomed." Apostle Twitty's vision is to "work diligently to build the Saints that the Saints might build the City. The first step in the building process is to get people to understand that "if you change the way you think you will change the way you live". With this vision in his heart, he is dedicated to "Reaching Outside The Walls" at whatever cost to seek and to save the lost.

In 1998, God gave Apostle Twitty a vision to establish R.O.T.W. and to write the vision as He had instructed and to make it plain. God told Apostle

Twitty to bring both the church and the world together to become the Kingdom of God. The mission of R.O.T.W. Ministries is to go out into the cities, cross over into other states, travel around the world and to other nations to restore, deliver, and to liberate God's people that they may declare unto themselves and others that they shall live and not die in the Kingdom of God.

God revealed to Apostle Twitty what the latter days would be like if he did what he believed was God. He told him how to bring the world into the Kingdom of God. He told him how to lead the 20th century church from its current state, how to dress her, arm her, and to equip her, that she may lose her traditional form and her religious status. Apostle Twitty was told to prepare for both a kingdom position and a priesthood role alongside men and women of God with the same Vision. The vision is to bring the body of Christ together as one, that we may go outside the walls and begin the work of the kingdom by gathering those who are lost in the system and have gotten entangled in the snares of the system. The "System" has failed us but the Kingdom will enable the world and the church to come together.

As founder of TRT Ministries, Apostle Twitty has authored the book Wait For It, which is based upon Isaiah 40:31: *"But they that wait upon the Lord shall renew their strength; they shall mount up with wings as eagles; they shall run, and not be weary; and they shall walk, and not faint."* This book is based upon everyday living and is backed by God's Word. He has taught several leadership series, but is most proud of the series "Making of a Leader" and _"The Nehemiah Strategic Planning Manual and Study Guide"_ Where he has taken the Word of God and the things of the spirit and made them applicable to the lives of everyday people seeking an understanding of God's plan for their life. Apostle Twitty has also published the book _"The Answer"_ which is based upon the book of Nehemiah. This book provides you with answers to the questions that you continue to seek God for as it relates to building your life, ministry, career and business. Apostle Twitty has authored _"The Revelation of Jesus Christ" Characteristics of the Seven Churches_, a dynamic book for learning about the seven churches of Asia Minor and the time that we are living in. Most recently he has authored the "P.M.S. (Power, Money & Sex) Book", which deals with the excitement and woes of relationships. It teaches you how to avoid bad relationships and ungodly soul-ties when choosing the mate that you were purposed by God to be with. The "31 Self-Strongholds" is the latest release by Apostle Twitty. It is a book that will give you insight into fighting the spiritual warfare that is the enemy within ourselves. We have dethroned God and blamed Him for losing our kingdom, but the kingdom of God lives within us and He gives us the authority and power to rule that kingdom. So we must determine as Joshua did, how to dethrone the strongholds that we have allowed into our kingdom, 1 stronghold at a time.

God has blessed Apostle Twitty to be heard on the radio and to be seen on several television shows. He is becoming more and more involved in his role in the communities as he expands the ROTW program, the **Community Awareness programs**. In spite of all that Apostle Twitty has accomplished, he always, without hesitation or reservation gives God the glory because he knows that nobody could have opened the doors that have been opened for him, but God.